CLEANING AND PREPARING GAMEFISH

Also by Monte Burch

CLEANING AND PREPARING GAMEFISH

Step-by-Step Instructions from Water to Table

Monte Burch

The Lyons Press
Guilford, Connecticut
An imprint of The Globe Pequot Press

The Lyons Press is an imprint of The Globe Pequot Press.

Printed in the United States of America

10 9 8 7 6 5 4 3 2 1

Library of Congress Cataloging-in-Publication Data is available on
file.

ISBN 1-58574-486-7

Contents

Introduction

Fish and shellfish have been staple foods since the beginning of mankind. Most of the world's larger cities were founded upon rivers, oceans, and lakes. These provided not only access to transportation but food as well. Fishing and collecting shellfish has been a way of life for many generations, and commercial fishing is still an important facet of the world's food supply.

For most of us, however, fishing is for sport, a means of enjoying a pleasant activity and at the same time collecting some food for the table. An old saying is, in fact, true—the family and friends who fish together tend to stay together. Fishing fortifies relationships, whether it's with family members, friends, or strangers sharing a riverbank. Taking youngsters fishing is especially important. Unfor-

Fish have provided food for humans since the beginning of time, and fishing is a traditional way of life for many cultures.

Fishing provides many pleasures to many people—regardless of age, experience, or position in life.

tunately, fewer families are going fishing these days. Parents are busy working overtime while kids are finding other interests to fill their lives. Fishing is also therapeutic for adults. Time on the water, away from business phones and petty stresses, helps cleanse the mind and soul of mental baggage that often impedes clear thinking and soul searching. Time spent fishing enables us to realign our priorities and get in touch with life's true values.

Fishing can provide many different types of satisfaction, from watching another angler land a big fish and sharing the experience, or teaching a novice how to cast or tie a knot. Even when the fish aren't biting, fishing can offer the rewards of being outdoors, on the water, observing and enjoying the limitless show nature provides: watching waterfowl or wild animals around the shorelines.

Fishing also doesn't discriminate. You don't need bulging muscles or agility. With a little help, a disabled child strapped in a wheelchair can land a 6-inch bluegill or bream with as much pride as anyone who lands a trophy for the record books.

The goal for many, however, is eating fish or shellfish. Dressed and prepared properly, fish and shellfish are exquisite. Improperly dressed, stored, transported, or prepared, fish and shellfish are poor in taste at the least, and dangerous to eat at the worst.

This book describes the methods of dressing and preparing the most common freshwater and saltwater fish and shellfish. The book also includes information on transporting fish as food items. Book chapters include information on preserving by smoking, pickling, or freezing, as well as basic cooking information. The final chapter also includes numerous fish and shellfish recipes. Many of these recipes are from our own kitchen or campfire, while others are garnered from friends, outfitters, and fishing guides.

Here's to the pleasure of fishing and the enjoyment of the many fine foods from the water.

CLEANING AND PREPARING GAMEFISH

CHAPTER 1

Catch and Release or Catch and Keep

The biggest decision for most anglers is whether to keep or release their catch. The choice depends on many factors and the first is legality. For instance, catching specific species or sizes of fish may be illegal in some areas, while others may be legal in that same area. Many sport fishermen like to release a fish as soon as it's caught. It's the thrill of the catch that inspires them, and they release a fish for the enjoyment of future fishermen. Tournament anglers keep their catch until after the weigh-in, and then the fish are released. This is still catch and release, although the numbers of fish that can die from the process depends greatly on how carefully the fish are handled during the weigh-in and then how they are later released. At many local tournaments, fish are simply dumped back into the water at the tournament weigh-in site. Some of the larger tournaments have live-release boats, such as those from Shimano. After the weigh-in, anglers place their fish in a 400-gallon livewell on Shimano's 28-foot modified pontoon boat. The boat then heads out onto the water to release the fish, distributing them over the lake rather than in just one locale.

The choice may also depend on the fishery. In areas with trophy fish, or on water with high angling pressure, catch and release may be the best choice or, in some cases, necessary. A prime example is catfishermen who take large numbers of big cats, don't eat all they catch, and then have to look for someone to give their catch to. Many of these big fish take many years to attain their size and their numbers are somewhat limited. On the other hand, another example is the two-acre pond below our house. It's a great bluegill pond, with lots of big hand-sized fish. Since lots of bluegills are

Many sport fishermen fish for the thrill of the catch, releasing the fish back into the water once it's caught.

taken from the pond on a regular basis it keeps the population in check.

Unfortunately, I think we've overdone catch and release. I'm not sure who coined the phrase, "selective harvest," but I think it was Doug Stange and the In-Fishermen crew. The term basically means take a few and leave a few, and for those who like to eat fish, it's a good rule to follow. The choice of what you take and leave depends on your personal feelings, your personal taste, and the legal limits.

Catch-and-release fishing is beneficial in some instances, but in others, such as with an overstocked pond, some fish must be kept to prevent overpopulation.

LANDING THE FISH

How you land the fish can make a difference as to whether it lives or dies. The best technique is turning the fish loose without even touching it. For small fish, slide your hand down the fishing line and slip the hook from its lip or jaw. Or, grab the hook with long-nosed pliers and twist the hook free. If the fish has swallowed the hook, cut the line. Don't attempt to remove the hook. In most instances the hook will rust out.

The best tactic to release small fish is to slip the hook from the fish without handling the fish.

A good landing net is necessary for larger fish. Make sure the net is wet before attempting to land the fish.

The next choice in landing the fish is to use a net. Some fish, such as toothy muskie or pike and big walleye, stripers and catfish, must be netted. I prefer to use a coated rubber net. Not only is it easier on the fish since it doesn't remove as much slime as a twine net, but it's also easier to get hooks out of. You'll get the fish back in the water much more quickly. Special nets that help support the entire length of the fish are also available for larger fish such as muskie. Make sure the net is wet before attempting to land the fish. Try to keep it from flopping and unhook it while it's still in the net. Don't set the net on the shore or on the bottom of the boat to unhook the fish. Two people should work quickly to remove the hooks.

Lower the net back into the water and hold the fish stationary until the fish catches its "breath." Remove the fish from the net and support it until it swims away under its own power. If the fish doesn't come around in a minute or two, keep it—it probably won't live.

If fishing in a river, support the fish by holding its tail, and then let the fish go in the slowest water available.

Never pick up a fish by the gill covers or eye sockets if you intend to release it. Don't touch the red gill tissue. A fish hooked in the gills, tongue, or eye, or a bleeding fish has very little chance of survival.

Where applicable, and if done properly, lipping the fish inflicts the least damage. Lipping is commonly done with bass, white bass, and other species, and I've even done it with walleye (but that's not suggested). A fish struggling in a net scrapes the protective mucus from its body, which can subject it to infection and a slow death over the next few days or weeks.

The "lippin'" method simply involves grasping the bass (or any other toothless fish) by the lower jaw in one quick, firm motion and lifting it into the boat while maintaining a tight grip on the jaw. Bending the jaw downward while lifting, holding, and removing the hooks paralyzes it and, in most instances, all struggling will cease. This makes hook removal much quicker and safer and there is no need to touch any other part of the fish's body.

Handling fish only by the lower jaw or "lip" eliminates the problem of trying to grasp a squirming, slimy fish by the body, which will invariably permanently injure it. Since fish are naturally hard to hold as they try to slip away, the angler will instinctively tighten his grip, causing internal injuries to a gamefish that he could have released alive.

Bass and other fish without sharp teeth can be subdued quite easily by "lipping." Grasping the lower jaw has a paralyzing effect and prevents struggling.

Care must be taken, however, to avoid the hook or hooks in the fish's mouth when using the "lippin'" method.

Naturally, you should never attempt to hand-land any fish that is still fighting. Carefully play each fish down and when the fish turns onto its side, insert your thumb into its mouth, away from the lure, tighten your grasp with the fingers beneath the jaw slightly flexed toward the fish, and lift it into the boat.

Handling gamefish that you plan to release by the jaw only will cause less damage than any other method. Never lay the fish on the carpet or floor of the boat because this also removes the protective covering.

If you want to release a fish right away, using barbless hooks can help. Barbless hooks are easier to remove and inflict fewer injuries. Many trout anglers simply reach into the water with forceps and remove the hook without ever touching the fish or removing it from the water.

If you want photographs, handle the fish as little as possible, and be sure to get your hands wet before touching it. Fish have a protective slime on their bodies, and wet hands will remove less of the slime than dry hands. While you have the fish out of the water, remember it can't breathe. Be as quick as possible, and then release it gently into the water.

In running water, hold the fish facing upstream, allowing water to pass over its gills to revive it. In a lake or pond, swirl the fish around in the water for the same effect.

Being caught stresses a fish and the longer you fight it, the more stressed it will be. Lengthy tussles with ultra light line and big fish are particularly detrimental. Making a fish fight for prolonged periods weakens it, so that even if it swims away, it may die later.

If you catch and release, use the strongest line you can get away with and don't prolong the battle.

TOURNAMENT FISHING

Tournament fishermen are motivated to keep their fish alive. Penalties are assessed for dead fish, and penalties can mean lost prize money. Tournament fishing boats have livewells that pump air and fresh water to keep the fish alive until they're brought to the weigh-in.

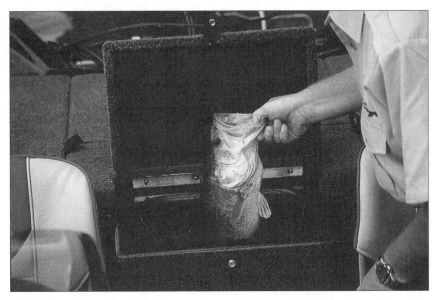

Boats with good livewells are used in tournaments to keep fish alive and healthy. Livewells can also be used to hold fish until you get home, if you are keeping them for eating.

Livewell additives can increase the fish's chance for survival. An effective livewell treatment should stabilize pH, detoxify ammonia, balance electrolytes, and create an artificial slime coating on the fish to replace what was lost when it was netted or otherwise touched.

Loading healthy fish into a plastic bag with a little water, then standing with the bag in a long line on shore in the hot sun is not good for the fish. Bagged fish will use up all the oxygen in a hurry, and toxins will start to build up in the water. Wait until the line is short and keep the fish in the livewell until you're ready to be weighed in.

In hot weather, fish get stressed because hot water doesn't hold as much oxygen as cooler water. Adding ice to the livewell can do more harm than good, however, if the ice is made from chlorinated water. Use a dechlorinating additive or make your ice from unchlorinated water.

With most livewells you can have fresh water and air pumped in all the time or you can set the switch to turn the livewells off and on at various timed intervals. In hot weather, run the livewell pumps continuously to keep your fish healthy.

CATCH AND KEEP

Catching fish is a blast and fish provide nutritious and tasty food. If you want to keep fish to eat, knowing how to care for your catch will make your experience even better. The warmer the conditions, the more critical proper handling becomes. An old saying goes, "the best fish is still flopping when you put it in the pan." You really don't have to be that finicky, but the flesh of fish is very delicate and will start to spoil quickly if it isn't treated properly. A roughly handled or stressed-out fish can start to spoil even before it dies. If you're fishing for food, use heavy enough tackle to keep the fight short and sweet. Get the fish into the boat as quickly as possible.

At that point the steps in ensuring healthy, tasty fish vary, depending on where you are located, the weather and temperature, and the type of fishing—for instance, from a bank, wading, or boating. The equipment you have available for keeping the catch alive is also important in what steps you take. And last, the fish species also often determines the best methods for keeping your catch.

Keeping them alive and healthy until you are ready to fillet them is the best way to ensure delicious fish in some species. If you're fishing from a boat, a livewell is an excellent method of keeping them alive and healthy. Many boats these days feature livewells with timers and aerators. If the weather is extremely hot, run the livewell constantly, rather than intermittently by the timer. One of the reasons I like my Charger bass boat is the large size of the livewells. They also pump water through coils wrapped around an onboard cooler, then around the livewell to help keep the water cool. When I head for home with fish in the livewell, I simply leave it running until I get there.

If you don't have a livewell, use a submersible basket to keep fish alive in the water until you are ready to go home. Fish baskets are great for the smaller panfish, especially bluegill when you're catching them on almost every cast. You can simply unhook the fish, open the basket, and drop it in headfirst. These baskets are better than stringers because you really don't have to handle the fish as much. It's important to keep the basket on a long cord deep

If keeping numbers of fish, fish baskets are better than stringers.

in the water, although not below the thermocline. This keeps the fish in a cooler environment and also prevents the basket from collapsing on the fish and preventing movement. Also be sure not to get the basket caught on an obstruction.

Back in the old days, my dad used a burlap "gunny sack" to keep his catch. He simply wove a piece of cord through the top to act as a drawstring and also as a tie rope for securing it to a riverbank tree or sprout. Dad even used the burlap sacks to transport his catfish and carp catches back home. The evaporative effect of the wet sack kept his catch cool and alive.

Stringers are, however, the most common method of keeping fish, yet they are usually not the best way, especially in hot weather. Fish on a stringer are more likely to die, and once dead, the flesh begins to deteriorate. Two types of stringers are used: line stringers and clip stringers. The less expensive line stringers are usually short and hard to use. The better line stringers, especially those used inshore by wading anglers, are long, to keep the catch away from the angler in case of sharks. These line stringers also have floats to keep fish from entangling on bottom structure. These are also the best

If using stringers, pin the fish to the stringer through the lower jaw rather than the gills to allow the fish to "breathe."

line stringers for freshwater anglers as well. The fish can be kept at a lower depth and farther from the bank or boat.

The stringers with individual clips are better than a single cord stringer for most freshwater situations, especially boating. They are more expensive, and since they are metal, tend to keep the fish deeper. The better stringers have clasps that swivel and turn, allowing the fish more mobility. These also allow for stringing individual fish on a single clip, alleviating the problem of line stringers when all the fish eventually get jammed up at the bottom of the stringer. Regardless of which stringer is used, stringers tend to be "drug" around behind the boat, often at high speeds when the angler forgets the stringer, and this also stresses the fish. Some fish, such as bass, are more excitable than others, such as catfish, and the more excitable fish often fight the stringer.

How you pin the fish to the stringer can make a great deal of difference in the length of time the fish will stay alive on it. The worst mistake most anglers make is threading the line or clips through the mouth and out the gills of the fish. This prevents the fish from using the natural breathing action of its gills and also creates an "open mouth" situation if the fish is caught in an obstruction or pulled behind the boat at faster speeds. As each fish is caught it should be threaded on the stringer through both lips. This allows the fish to breath by keeping the mouth closed and working the gills. Threading through just one lip or through the mouth and gills can drown the fish. When you move the boat, pick the stringer entirely out of the water and place it down in the boat. If going a long distance, place the stringer of fish in a bucket filled with lake water.

One of the biggest problems of fish on a stringer is having old brother turtle come along and snatch your catch. Or if saltwater fishing, you may just have a shark breathing down your neck while you innocently wade along.

Fish boxes can also be used for temporarily holding fish, but, again, they should be placed in a well-aerated, shady, or cool place. The more excitable fish don't do as well in confinement. The amount of time to hold the fish varies. Catfish, carp, and other bottom feeders taken from some waters, particularly in the summer, often have a musty flavor. They can be kept in the fish box for five to seven days to help purge the taste.

Another method is to kill the fish immediately, then gut or fillet it. My good friend Jerry Thies fishes his private bass lake with a battery-powered electric fillet knife plugged into his trolling motor battery. When he catches a bass he wants to keep, he kills the fish with a whack on the head with a short club, then fillets it, rinses the fillet blades and cutting board, and wipes them down with moist towelettes. The fillets are placed in plastic locking bags and then on ice in a cooler. Within a matter of minutes, Jerry is back to fishing.

When wade fishing for trout, the fish are sometimes placed on a stringer. More often they are simply gutted, removing the gills and kidney along the backbone, then placed in a creel. If you carry more than one fish, don't allow them to touch each other. Place them on dry grass with grass between them. Do not use moss or green grass since it heats up and can cause deterioration. Cabela's carries a dandy Classic Split-Willow Creel that has the traditional look. Their Arcti-Creel, made of Scottish flax water bag canvas, uses evaporation to greatly reduce the temperature to keep fish in excellent condition.

Regardless of the methods of caring for the fish, if it is deeply hooked, do not attempt to remove the hook. Cut it free, leaving a

Fish boxes are an excellent means of temporarily holding fish.

bit of line attached. You can remove the hook later, when you clean the fish.

A tactic used for many species is to place them on ice as soon as they've been caught. This is especially important with most saltwater and some freshwater species. I prefer to kill crappie with a blow to the back of the head using a "billy" and then place them in plastic locking bags, on ice. If you fish with several anglers and your state requires each must keep his own catch, write the anglers names on the bags to make it easy to keep the catches separate. The fish should not be placed down in the water, but kept up on the ice.

Many saltwater fish are gaffed, then immediately placed on ice. Capt. Robert Trosset of Key West, Florida, says adding salt to the ice helps keep the meat fresher. He starts with a bit of rock salt, then adds salt water as needed. It's important to keep the ice-slush replenished and keep the fish down in it.

Some fish, particularly the oily fishes such as white bass, striped bass, many sea fish, and the rough fish such as carp, are best bled and gutted before you place them on ice. You can do this by first

Fillet or clean the fish as soon as it's caught. (Make sure you follow game regulations.)

cutting the artery near the tail or a large artery in the isthmus between the gills, and then slicing the belly and eviscerating it. If it's against the law in your state or province to dump fish guts back into the water, place them in plastic garbage bags that can also be kept in the cooler until you can properly dispose of them.

Regardless, once you have killed a fish, it must be dressed immediately. According to information from *Proper Field Dressing and Handling of Wild Game and Fish,* published by Penn State College of Agricultural Sciences, and compiled by Catherine N. Cutter:

> Once they have been killed, fish should be cleaned promptly, since enzymes, bacteria and oxygen all begin working to diminish the quality of the meat. Enzymes will spoil the meat rapidly and cause "off" flavors. Enzymes in living seafood help to build tissue, contract and relax muscles and digest food. After harvest, they continue to work, digesting or breaking down the flesh, softening it and lowering its quality. Enzymes also produce more food for bacteria, which increases the rate of spoilage.
>
> Bacteria are the major cause of seafood spoilage. Millions of bacteria live on the surface, on the gills, and in the gut of living fish and shellfish. After harvest, they invade the flesh through the gills, along blood vessels, and directly through the skin and belly cavity lining. These bacteria grow and multiply, producing the "fishy" smelling and tasting compounds associated with old seafood. If food-poisoning bacteria are present, they can multiply and cause illness.
>
> Finally, oxygen in the air attacks the oils in seafood and causes rancidity, "off" odors and "off" flavors. This commonly occurs in fatty fish such as salmon and mackerel.

TRANSPORTING FISH

If it is not possible to transport the fish alive, they should be killed, gutted and/or filleted for transportation. If possible, rinse the fish in cold, clean water to remove all bacteria, blood, and digestive enzymes. Dry the surface using a clean, soft cloth or better yet, paper towels. This drying step is extremely important because water is the cause of most of the problems with cleaned fish. Place the fish or fillets in sealable plastic bags. Make sure they are kept on ice, but not down in the melting water from the ice. Freshly caught fish should be cooled as quickly as possible, down to between 35 and 40 degrees F. to prevent bacterial growth. If you are transporting them by boat, keep the cooler in the shade, or cover it with a blanket or other insulator. If you have been fishing all day, and have a long drive home, dump the water off the ice and replenish with fresh ice. Always use fresh, clean ice. Old or dirty ice may harbor bacteria.

TRANSPORTING SALTWATER FISH AND SHELLFISH

Many of us don't live seaside, yet would like to bring home our catch fresh. Seafood can be safely transported long distances for several days, if handled properly. The key is to keep it cold. The colder the temperature, the slower the spoilage rate. This requires a good, well-insulated cooler of the appropriate size. You will also need flaked or crushed iced and rock or table salt. Mix a salt-ice solution of ½ pound of salt for each five pounds of ice in a separate container. The cooler should first be lined with about three inches of the ice-salt mixture. Place a rack in the bottom of the cooler to keep the fish up out of the water that accumulates from the melting ice. Place a layer of fish in the cooler, and then a layer of ice.

For the quickest cooling, fish should be dressed, or headed, gilled, and eviscerated. Large fish, including tuna, should have been gutted and bled immediately after being caught. If fish are to be transported whole, pack the body cavity with ice. It may be best on large fish, such as tuna, to first cut them into smaller pieces that will fit in the cooler. Do not wrap the eviscerated fish.

For seafood such as shrimp, head them, but leave the shells on and place them in a heavy plastic bag. Shucked shellfish should also be placed in heavy-duty plastic bags. Cover the seafood with at least three inches of ice-salt and close the cooler and the drain plug. Place the cooler in the coolest portion of your car. If traveling overnight, drain off the melted water and ice and add more ice-salt mixture.

LIVE SHELLFISH

You can also transport live shellfish, but it takes a bit more effort to ensure the safety of the food. A well-insulated cooler is also needed for this chore. Place a three- to four-inch layer of ice in the bottom of the cooler. Place a piece of foam or cardboard with holes punched in it over the ice. Place live crabs or oysters on top of the cardboard or foam. Partially close the cooler lid. This provides a cold temperature that keeps the crabs inactive. A temperature of 40 to 50 degrees F. is best for crabs, but you should limit the holding period to one day. Clams can also be transported in this manner, but the temperature should be kept at 35 to 45 degrees F. Do not hold oysters or clams more than two to three days in this manner.

It's extremely important to make sure live shellfish are still alive when you arrive home. Do not use any fresh seafood that has died in transport. Live crabs will have movement of their legs. The shells of clams and live oysters should be tightly closed, or close when the shell is tapped.

It's also important to regularly clean and freshen your cooler. Scrub with a solution of baking soda and a little water, and then clean with a hose and fresh water. Allow the cooler to stay open until thoroughly air-dried. An open box of baking soda can be kept in the cooler to keep it smelling fresh when not in use.

Back at home, I like to soak all fish in salt water for about 15 minutes, and then rinse thoroughly in cold water. The fish are then ready for the pan, preserving, or freezing.

FRESH FISH AND SHELLFISH

Following are a few things to look for to assure quality, safe meat— whether it's fish you've caught yourself or the catch of the day from the fish market:

1. Bright red gills. The gills should not be gray, brown, green, or dull pink. They should also be free from slime.
2. Clear, not milky eyes. The eyes should be bright and slightly protruding. The eyes sink back in the eye sockets as the fish begins to decompose.
3. No offensive smell. Fresh fish should have no "fishy" smell.
4. Firm, yet elastic flesh. The flesh should bounce back at a touch. And, it should not be separated from the bone. Fillets should also be elastic yet firm with no drying or browning around the edges.

5. Bright and shiny skin. The skin should not be dull. Scales should be adhered tightly in place. The markings or color pattern fade as the fish deteriorates.
6. Bright red blood streak in the intestinal cavity. The streak should not be brown or dark red.

Live crabs and lobsters should have movement of the legs. The tail of a lobster should not hang down, but should curl up when picked up. Oysters and clams in the shell should be tightly closed, or should close tightly when the shell is tapped.

Shucked oysters should not have a great deal of liquid and should be a creamy or clear color with a plump look. They will have a slight odor. Fresh scallops should also not have excessive liquid and should have a sweet odor. Sea scallops should be slightly pink, orange, or creamy white. Bay scallops should be creamy white. Shrimp should have firm meat, with a mild odor. Shrimp should not be slimy and should have a natural color. Shrimp that have black spots or that are bright red or pink should be avoided.

If purchasing frozen fish or shellfish, make sure the meat is frozen solid and free of any ice crystals. Ice crystals indicate the results of thawing and then refreezing. There should be no freezer burn, and the meat should be well wrapped.

Nutrition and Safety

Fish is good for you! In fact, nutrition experts, including the American Heart Association, recommend at least two to three servings of fish per week. Unfortunately, studies show Americans eat approximately 15 pounds of fish per year as opposed to over 90 pounds of poultry and around 160 pounds of red meat.

The flesh of fish is low in cholesterol as well as the saturated fats that raise blood cholesterol levels. The fats found in fish, however, are extremely high in polyunsaturates. Fish oil contains omega-3 fatty acids. Omega-3 refers to the place in the fat molecule where two carbon atoms are linked together by a double bond—in this case between the third and fourth carbon. The two main omega-3 fats found in marine oils are eicosapentaenoic acid (EPA) and docosahexaenoic acid (DHA). Experts are discovering that these unsaturated fats with their acids offer numerous health benefits. They alter the chemical makeup of blood, increasing levels of HDL (the cholesterol that helps prevent heart attacks). They decrease levels of LDL (the cholesterol that adds to health problems). They also decrease triglycerides. A study released 17 January 2001, in the *Journal of The American Medical Association,* states that the intake of fish and omega-3 fatty acids can lower the risk of stroke in women.

Other studies have shown omega-3 fats also influence the blood platelet aggregation. Platelets are the constituent in blood that helps it clot. This is important for wound healing. When the blood becomes too sticky, however, it can further the progression of heart disease, especially in vessels injured with plaque formation. Research indicates that EPA in particular helps reduce the stickiness of blood platelets. Fish oils also appear to help stabilize heart rhythm, a concern to people recovering from heart attacks.

The fatty acids found in fish help prevent blood platelets from sticking together, allowing them to more readily pass through tiny blood vessels. Omega-3 fatty acids are also used in the human body to produce prostaglandins, which are used in numerous ways, including fighting inflammation and in other functions of the immune system. Fish oils contain EPA, which may assist in the development of prostaglandins and other substances that can help relieve the painful symptoms of rheumatoid arthritis. Omega-3 may also fight common skin diseases, such as eczema and psoriasis.

All types of fish provide an abundance of nutrients. Fish is especially rich in water-soluble B vitamins. The more oily fish provide lots of vitamin A, D, and K. Fish also supply an abundance of minerals including calcium, iodine, magnesium, copper, fluoride, phosphorus, potassium, zinc, selenium, and iron. All are major keys to good health.

Because they must pack so much muscle on a tiny skeleton, fish provide more protein per serving than most other meats.

Shellfish, which includes both crustaceans and mollusks, provide a very high-quality protein per serving. The protein is extremely low in fat, but has more omega-3 fatty acids than other low-fat fish. Many varieties of shellfish, however, have somewhat high levels of cholesterol, and in the past have not been recommended for persons with high serum cholesterol. It is now felt, however, that although shellfish have higher cholesterol levels than finfish, they can be consumed in moderation in the same quantities permitted in other low-cholesterol diets including red meat and fowl.

Shellfish, however, are quite low in the saturated fats that raise blood cholesterol levels. All shellfish also contain the omega-3 fatty acids and have fewer calories than other meat proteins. Shellfish provide a wealth of minerals including phosphorus, fluoride, calcium, iodine, magnesium, iron, and zinc. Shellfish are also rich in vitamins, especially the B vitamins: thiamine, niacin, and riboflavin.

Not all fish and shellfish, however, are equal in the nutrients they provide. The higher fat, cold-water species including salmon, sardines, and lake trout and saltwater species such as tuna, albacore, and mackerel, contain higher levels of omega-3 fats than freshwater fish. Following is a chart with the nutrients for a wide variety of species.

The good news is fish is good for you. Fish flesh is low in cholesterol as well as saturated fats that raise cholesterol levels. Fish also contains Omega-3 fatty acids, which offer many other health benefits.

Nutrition Chart

Species	Measure	Protein (g)	Energy (Kcal)	Fat (g)	Cholesterol (mcg)	Saturated Fat (g)	Monounsaturated (g)	Polyunsaturated (g)
Catfish, Channel, breaded & fried	3 oz.	15.38	195	11.33	69	2.795	4.769	2.826
Clam, raw	3 oz.	10.85	63	0.82	29	0.08	0.068	0.24
Cod, Pacific, cooked	3 oz.	19.51	89	0.69	40	0.088	0.089	0.266
Crab, Alaska King, cooked	3 oz.	16.45	82	1.31	45	0.113	0.157	0.456
Crab, Blue, cooked	3 oz.	17.17	87	1.5	85	0.194	0.238	0.578
Flatfish, cooked	3 oz.	20.54	99	1.3	58	0.309	0.201	0.549
Haddock, cooked	3 oz.	20.6	95	0.79	63	0.142	0.128	0.263
Halibut, cooked	3 oz.	22.69	119	2.5	35	0.354	0.822	0.799
Herring, Atlantic, pickled	3 oz.	12.07	223	15.31	11	2.025	10.161	1.428
Lobster, Northern, cooked	3 oz.	17.43	83	0.5	61	0.091	0.136	0.077
Oyster, Eastern, wild, raw	6 med.	5.92	57	2.07	45	0.648	0.264	0.813
Ocean Perch, Atlantic, cooked	3 oz.	20.3	103	1.78	46	0.266	0.681	0.465
Pollock, Walleye, cooked	3 oz.	19.98	96	0.95	82	0.196	0.148	0.445
Rockfish, Pacific, cooked	3 oz.	20.43	103	1.71	37	0.403	0.38	0.505
Roughy, Orange, cooked	3 oz.	16.02	76	0.77	22	0.02	0.523	0.014
Salmon, Chinook, smoked	3 oz.	15.55	100	3.67	20	0.79	1.721	0.846
Salmon, Sockeye, cooked	3 oz.	23.21	184	9.32	74	1.629	4.497	2.048
Scallop, breaded & fried	6 large	16.81	200	10.17	57	2.482	4.183	2.656
Shrimp, breaded & fried	6 large	9.63	109	5.53	80	0.939	1.715	2.288
Swordfish, cooked	3 oz.	21.58	132	4.37	43	1.195	1.684	1.005
Trout, Rainbow, farmed, cooked	3 oz.	20.63	144	6.12	58	1.789	1.782	1.981
Tuna, Yellowfin, cooked	3 oz.	25.47	118	1.04	49	0.256	0.167	0.309

Safety Concerns

Given that fish are good for you, it's important to also understand that fish and shellfish from some waters may contain chemicals that could pose health risks, especially if eaten in large quantities. Fish and, especially, shellfish from polluted waters can cause birth defects, liver damage, cancer, and other serious health problems. Some chemical pollutants, such as mercury and PCBs, can pose greater risks to women of childbearing age, pregnant women, nursing mothers, and young children. This group should be especially careful to greatly reduce or avoid eating fish or shellfish taken from polluted waters.

Chemical pollutants in the water may come from many sources. They come from factories and sewage treatment plants you can easily see. Chemical pollutants also come from sources that you can't easily see such as chemical spills or runoff from city streets and farm fields. Pollutants are also carried long distance in the air. Fish may be exposed to chemical pollutants in the water and the food they eat. They may take up some of the pollutants into their bodies. The pollutants are found in the skin, fat, internal organs, and sometimes muscle tissue of fish. For instance, Reuters Health reported that more than eight out of ten fish in a Virginia sampling showed troublesome concentrations of BDE—brominated diphenyl ether—an organic pollutant that comes from treated sewage sludge farmers spread on crops. Numerous brown bullheads from the Detroit River have been found to have skin cancers and liver tumors from exposure to polynuclear aromatic hydrocarbons found in river sediments.

You can reduce the risk of eating fish containing chemical pollutants by following several steps suggested by the Environmental Protection Agency.

The first step is to determine if the water is polluted. It's almost impossible to tell if a body of water is polluted simply by looking at it. Nevertheless, there are ways to find out. Look to see if warning signs are posted along the water's edge. If warning signs are present, follow the advice printed on them. Even if you don't see warning signs, call your local or state health or environmental protection department and ask for their advice. Ask them if there are any advisories on the kinds or sizes of fish that may be eaten from the waters in which you plan to fish. You can also ask about fishing advisories at local sporting goods shops or bait shops where fishing licenses are sold. Most state fish and game departments also issue advisories as well.

You also can't look at a fish and tell if it contains chemical pollutants—the only way to tell if a fish contains harmful levels of chemical pollutants is to have it tested in a laboratory. Therefore, if a body of water has not been tested, follow these guidelines to reduce health risks from eating fish that might contain small amounts of chemical pollutants.

If you eat game fish such as lake trout, salmon, walleye, and bass, eat the smaller, younger fish (taken within legal length limits). They are less likely to contain harmful levels of pollutants than larger, older fish.

Eat panfish such as bluegill, perch, stream trout, and smelt. They feed on insects and other aquatic life and are less likely to contain high levels of harmful pollutants.

Eat fewer fatty fish, such as lake trout, or fish that feed on the bottoms of lakes and streams, such as catfish and carp. These fish are more likely to contain higher levels of chemical pollutants.

The method you use to clean fish can also reduce the amount of pollutants that might be present. Clean and dress the fish as soon as possible. It's a good idea to remove the skin, fat, and internal organs (where harmful pollutants are most likely to accumulate) before you cook the fish. As an added precaution, remove and throw away the head, guts, kidneys, and liver. Fillet the fish and cut away the fat and skin before you cook it. Trim away the fatty tissue to reduce the level of some pollutants.

The cooking method can also make a difference in the kinds and amounts of chemical pollutants remaining in the fish. Fish should be properly prepared and grilled, baked, or broiled. By letting the fat drain away, you can remove pollutants stored in the fatty parts.

You should also avoid or reduce the amount of fish drippings or broth that you use to flavor a meal. These drippings may contain higher levels of pollutants.

Eat less fried or deep-fat fried fish because frying seals any chemical pollutants that might be in the fish's fat into the portion that you will eat.

If you like smoked fish, it is best to fillet the fish and remove the skin before it is smoked.

Mercury Poisoning

Mercury is one of the more common pollutants. At least 42 states have issued advisories for mercury. In addition, the Food and Drug Administration (FDA) has issued advisories on mercury in fish bought from stores and restaurants, including ocean and coastal fish, as well as other types of commercial fish.

Mercury is a natural occurring toxic trace element found in air, water, soil, and rocks. It is a member of a group of elements known as heavy metals and is used in household and commercial products and industrial processes. Mercury is converted in the environment by microorganisms into the organic form, methylmercury, which is highly toxic.

Mercury emissions occur from both natural and man-made sources. Man-made sources account for the majority of all emissions, many of which can be controlled: coal and oil burning, commercial/industrial boilers, lead smelting, cement and lime kilns, crematories, dental amalgam preparation and disposal, dwelling demolition (switches, fluorescent lights, some headlights, and batteries), evaporation of mercury from landfills, garbage incinerators, hazardous waste incinerators, industrial wastewater treatment plants, and wood burning. Although the EPA and many state agencies are working to reduce mercury pollution, methylmercury is very persistent and it will be several years before methylmercury levels in fish and the environment are reduced.

There has been considerable discussion and concern about the level of exposure to methylmercury that may have negative health effects on humans during a lifetime. In 1999, Congress directed the EPA to contract with the National Research Council (NRC) of the National Academy of Sciences to evaluate the available data on the health effects of methylmercury. The NRC published their report, "Toxicological Effects of Methylmercury" in 2000. The EPA agreed with their conclusions and developed the methylmercury criterion of 0.3 ppm (300ppb) in fish tissue that should not be exceeded to protect the health of consumers of noncommercial freshwater fish.

Methylmercury bioaccumulates in the muscles of fish (not the fat). For this reason, cleaning and dressing, as well as cooking methods, do not remove mercury from the fish. Trimming the fat or grilling will not reduce mercury levels in the food. The primary environmental route of exposure to methylmercury is from eating contaminated fish.

Mercury poisoning can damage the central nervous system, kidneys, and liver in humans and can impair child development.

Methylmercury becomes progressively more concentrated as it moves up the food chain and can pose a health risk to humans and wildlife that consume large quantities of mercury-contaminated fish. Smaller fish have lower levels of contamination than larger fish of the same species. Eat the smaller legal fish and release big fish to fight another day. Select fish such as bluegill, other sunfish, and channel catfish, which are lower on the food chain and therefore contain lower levels of methylmercury.

For more information contact: U.S. Environmental Protection Agency, Office of Water, Fish Contamination Program (4305), 401 M. Street, SW, Washington, DC 20460, www.epa.gov/ost/fishadvice

Scombroid Poisoning

Scombroid poisoning is a type of foodborne illness caused by the consumption of scombroid and scombroid-like marine fish species that have begun to spoil with the growth of particular types of bacteria. Scombroid poisoning usually is not a severe or long-term illness, and prevention is not difficult, yet occurrences continue throughout the world, according to the Clemson University Service of South Carolina. The principal threat is from fresh fish, but the illness can result from consumption of certain frozen, cooked, or canned fish products. Fish most commonly involved are members of the scombridae family (tunas and mackerels) and a few non-scombridae relatives (bluefish, dolphin or mahi-mahi, and amberjack). The suspected toxin is an elevated level of histamine generated by bacterial breakdown of substances in the muscle protein. This natural spoilage process is thought to release additional by-products, which cause the toxic effect. Freezing, cooking, smoking, curing, or canning does not destroy the potential toxins. Scombroid poisoning cannot be detected by appearance or taste. Proper handling of fish is the best safeguard. Potential scombrotoxic fish should receive special care in handling, washing and proper dressing, and should be immediately refrigerated or frozen to prevent bacterial growth and spoilage. Studies have shown that toxic histamine levels can be generated within less than six to twelve hours of exposure without ice or refrigeration. Prevention is simple and preferable to treatment, which is similar to that used for allergic reactions. Common advice from physicians includes treatments with antihistamines.

Scombroid poisoning symptoms can also be confused with an allergy or other form of food poisoning, including ciguatera, another form of marine fish poisoning.

Ciguatera

Ciguatera illness generally occurs in the tropical regions of the world. Presently, ciguatera is relatively rare in the United States and occurs less often than many common bacterial food poisonings, but it still ranks among the top four annually reported seafood-borne illnesses.

Ciguatera occurs in marine waters near tropical reefs. Potentially any tropical marine fish participating in the food chain with ciguatoxin could become ciguatoxic, but documented illnesses and some recent analyses indicate certain fish are more suspect. The fish with the worst reputation in the Caribbean are amberjacks and other jacks, moray eels, and barracuda. Fish with questionable reputations are hogfish, scorpion fishes, certain triggerfish, and certain snapper and groupers. Initial symptoms are gastrointestinal, including nausea, cramping, and vomiting. This is followed by neurological discomforts: headaches, flushing, muscular aching and weakness, tingling and numbing sensation of the lips, tongue and mouth, dizziness, muscle pain, and joint pain. Victims usually recover within a few days, but severe neurological disorders may persist for months and sometimes for years.

Consult a physician, explaining your concern, type and amount of food eaten, and when the symptoms began. Rapid diagnosis by a physician and follow-up treatment are important.

Vibrio vulnificus

According to Clemson Extension Service of South Carolina, about 20 million Americans eat raw oysters. For some people, however, eating raw oysters can cause serious illness or even death. The cause is *Vibrio vulnificus,* a bacterium that occurs in warm marine waters. *V. vulnificus* infections are transmitted to humans either through open wounds in contact with sea water or by eating certain improperly cooked or raw shellfish. *V. vulnificus* is most likely to be present during warm months. While not a threat to healthy people, *V. vulnificus* can cause sudden chills, fever, nausea, vomiting, blood poisoning, and death within two days in people with certain medical conditions.

Norwalk Virus

Ingestion of raw or insufficiently steamed clams and oysters also poses a high risk of infection from the Norwalk virus, a cause of viral gastroenteritis or the stomach "bug," according to Clemson Extension Service. It is estimated that Norwalk viruses are responsible for about one-third of the cases of viral gastroenteritis not involving the 6- to 24-month age group. Approximately 181,000 cases occur annually with no known associated deaths. Norwalk and Norwalk-like viruses have been associated with outbreaks on cruise ships, in communities, camps, schools, institutions, and families. Foods such as raw oysters, cake frosting, and salads, as well as drinking water, have been implicated.

Additional Safeguards

Fish and shellfish must be kept cold to ensure the best quality. Keep your refrigerator temperature at 32 to 38 degrees F. and your freezer at 0 degrees F. or colder. Do not refreeze previously frozen fish.

Shellfish, which includes mollusks and crustaceans, such as crawfish, also offer many benefits.

Make sure you wash your hands with soap and water before serving or eating food. Serve cooked products on clean plates with clean utensils and clean hands. Never place cooked foods on a dish that has held raw products unless the dish is first washed with soap and hot water. Hold hot foods above 140 degree F. and cold foods below 40 degree F.

Yellow Grubs

For some anglers, the delight of catching a keeper-size fish turns to dejection when the filleting process uncovers yellow grubs. The Missouri Department of Conservation Fisheries Management Specialist Dale Cornelius says that while grubs may not look appetizing, they will not ruin your catch. Fish have always been hosts for yellow grubs. He suspects the parasites are being found more often because increasingly anglers are filleting their catches and the filleting process uncovers the yellow grubs.

"The yellow grub is a common parasite that can affect any species of fish. In the past people probably didn't notice them because they would scale and clean the fish then cook them without skinning or filleting them. Now that many people filet or skin their fish, they have a greater chance of seeing the parasites that have burrowed into the flesh of the fish," says Cornelius.

According to Cornelius, the yellow grub parasite begins its complex life cycle in fish-eating birds. Adult grubs lay eggs in the throats and mouths of the birds. Those eggs are expelled when the birds feed. Larvae emerge from eggs and burrow into the bodies of snails, where they continue to grow and change form. Once a grub leaves the snail, it attaches to a fish and burrows into its flesh. The cycle then repeats itself when a fish-eating bird eats the infected fish. Anglers who catch fish that have yellow grubs may either remove them from the fish or thoroughly cook the fish.

Cornelius says because chemical treatments are not economically feasible and the grubs are harmless, there is no need to attempt to rid your pond of them. But for those insistent on attempting to control the parasites, stocking redear sunfish may be the solution. The sunfish eat snails and could possibly decrease a pond's grub population. Redear sunfish, which can grow up to 12 inches long, also are excellent eating.

Tools

Dressing fish such as trout the moment they are caught requires nothing more than a sharp knife. Add a canoe paddle as a "table" for filleting walleye for a shore lunch and you can see how simple it is and how few tools are actually required for dressing and preparing many fish species. Whether at home or in camp, you can dress and clean most fish with just a few tools.

A sharp knife and a smooth surface is all that's required to clean most fish.

KNIVES

Naturally, the required tool is a knife. I've dressed panfish with a pocketknife in an emergency, but fillet knives, designed specifically for the purpose, make the chore easier and quicker. Fillet knives are available in a wide variety of shapes, sizes, and materials. Quality varies a great deal as well. Poor quality fillet knives are made of metal that won't sharpen and won't hold an edge. These knives can even be dangerous because they make you push and work harder, which can result in a slip and a nasty cut.

The blades of the better quality fillet knives are made of rust-resistant, high carbon, stainless steel. Fillet knives are available with straight- or serrated-edge blades. Straight-edge blades are fine for panfish, but the serrated ones work better on larger fish and on those fish that require cutting through heavy scales. Kershaw has an excellent fillet knife that comes with two removable blades: a straight and a combination straight- and serrated-edge blade. Both blades and the knife are enclosed in a Cordura case. The blades can quickly and easily be switched as desired by flicking a thumb button.

The proper knives can make the chore easier. Shown is a wide selection of fillet knives available from Berkley, Buck, Gerber, Katz, Intruder, Shimano, and Kershaw.

The removable blade knife from Kershaw has both a straight and serrated blade with a case to hold both.

The blades on fillet knives are also available in several lengths. If you normally fillet small and pan-sized fish, the shorter blades of six inches are perfect and aren't as awkward to carry on your belt. For larger fish, you'll need longer blades. Knives are available with blades up to twelve inches in length. Also available from Kershaw is their seven-step adjustable fillet knife. This Kershaw knife allows you to vary the blade length to fillet just about any sized catch with a single knife. The blade adjusts from five and one-half through nine inches in seven different positions by merely pushing on a lever on the handle.

Fillet knives are available with either wood or molded handles. Wooden handles are traditional, and still popular in presentation knives. Knives with molded handles, however, are becoming more popular. The molded handles allow for either molded-in grips or, in many of the better knives, a soft-grip handle. Both provide a better hold when the handles are wet. Fillet knives are also available with fixed blades, the most common, or with folding blades. The folding versions are like giant pocketknives. If you purchase a folding-blade fillet knife, make sure the blade locks securely in place.

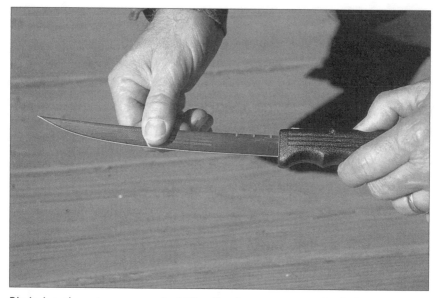

Blade length varies a great deal. The Kershaw seven-step knife has adjustable blade length.

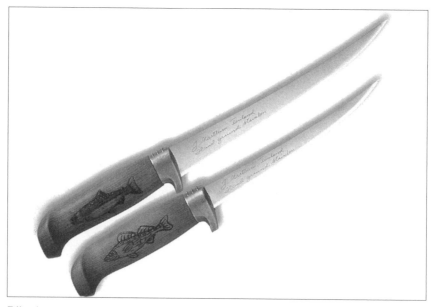

Fillet knives are available with traditional wood or molded handles.

Folding-blade fillet knives are easier to store in tackle boxes. You can even carry them in your pocket.

Most fixed-blade knives also have a hole in the back of the handle so you can add a cord to loop around your wrist. You'll avoid dropping the knife in the water when you use it on a boat or fish-cleaning station that is located over water.

Many fillet knives come with a sheath which may be leather, Cordura, or molded plastic. The latter has quickly become the most

Most fillet knives are available with leather, Cordura, or plastic sheaths.

common. Regardless of the material, make sure the knife snaps down or fits snugly in the case so it can't fall out. Most of the plastic cases also have an opening in the bottom so moisture can drain or evaporate.

Knife Care

The carbon content in the blade determines how quickly the blade may corrode if not properly cared for. Full stainless steel rarely corrodes. It's a good idea to wipe a light coating of oil on any blade before storing it. If using the knife in salt water, immediately rinse with fresh water after use, then wipe a coat of oil on the blade.

Knife Sharpening

Like all knives, it's extremely important to keep fillet knives sharp. Dull knives can cause you to exert more force when cutting into the fish. The blade may slip and cut *you* instead.

Due to the thinness of the blades, it's extremely important to properly sharpen fillet knives and not allow the blade to overheat during the sharpening process. One of the worst mistakes is attempting to sharpen a fillet knife on a dry electric grinder. You'll ruin the blade before you get started.

A number of sharpening devices are available ranging from manual ceramic sticks, diamond sticks, and hones. One of the easiest I've used is the Deluxe Knife Sharpener from Intruder. It makes anyone an instant expert sharpener in ten seconds. The sharpener features a full-length protective strap and large grip handle that makes sharpening easy and safe. Accusharp blades are both reversible and replaceable, featuring a tough, rust-proof design and Diamond Honed Tungsten Carbide Sharpeners. Intruder's Sharp-N-Easy features strong, locked-in carbide sharpeners and a protective handle for easy use. The MultiEdge Professional Diamond Hone Knife Sharpener from Chef'sChoice is a great manual sharpener that can be used for both straight and serrated blades. The sharpener features two stages for sharper, longer-lasting edges. The 100-percent diamond abrasives optimize sharpening power and precision roller guides ensure accurate angle control for foolproof and easy sharpening.

Several electric hones are also available that can make the chore easier and quicker. The Chef'sChoice Edge Select Professional #120 Diamond Hone Knife Sharpener from EdgeCraft Corporation is one

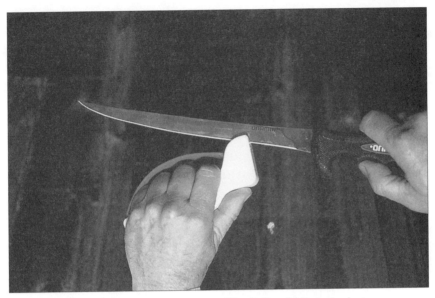

The handy Intruder Sharp-N-Easy keeps fillet knives finely honed.

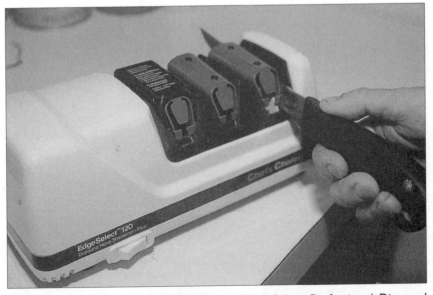

Back at camp or home, the Chef'sChoice Edge Select Professional Diamond Hone Knife Sharpener is hard to beat.

of the best I've tested. It features patented precision guides for accurate control of the sharpening angle. You'll get foolproof results. The multi-stage design utilizes 100-percent diamond abrasives in stage one and two, and a unique stropping and polishing in stage three, providing a triple-bevel razor edge quickly and easily.

Another good choice is the water reservoir Craftsman Utility Sharpener. It works on the same principle as the old-fashioned foot-operated, water-grindstone of the past. It should be used with a fine grit, aluminum-oxide grinding wheel.

Fillet knives are designed to be long-lasting and sturdy when used for their intended purpose. They are, however, for the most part thin and should not be misused. A fillet knife should not be used as a screwdriver, chisel, can opener, or pry bar. Never hammer on the back of the blade. Don't use them as throwing knives. Strong twisting, scraping, or pounding forces may damage the blade—and cause serious injury.

Electric Fillet Knives

Nothing makes fillet work easier than an electric fillet knife. Bass, walleye, crappie, even catfish are quickly and easily filleted. I've

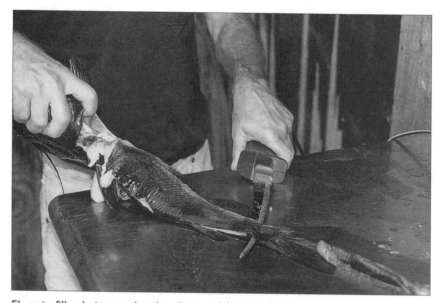

Electric fillet knives make the chore of filleting quick and easy, even on larger fish. They're available in 110- and 12-volt models.

had a Mister Twister fillet knife for many years and I really don't know how many fish it's dressed. It's available either as a 110-volt or 12-volt model that can be used in camp, running off a boat or automobile battery. I've also used the American Angler fillet knife with its pointed blades; it's great for saltwater fish.

Other Knives

You may also need additional tools if you work up larger fish by planking or steaking. You'll need butcher knives and cleavers for this task. These knives and cleavers should also be stainless steel, especially if you work with saltwater fish.

GLOVES

Fillet gloves can be used to protect your hands, not only from the knife but also from the extremely sharp edges of gill plates on fish such as walleye and white bass. The Intruder Stainless Steel Fillet Gloves are made of a blend of stainless steel core fiber for strength and cut resistance and hi-tech wrappings of an interwoven

Fish-cleaning gloves can protect your hands from a slip with the fillet knife as well as from handling fish with sharp teeth or fins.

polyester and vinyl material for comfort, resistance to stains and odors, and easy washing. FDA/USDA-approved materials meet rigid food service industry standards. Many other companies offer fish cleaning/gripping gloves as well.

CUTTING SURFACES

You'll need cutting surfaces that are easily cleaned on which to dress fish. For filleting and scaling, a wooden board is hard to beat. And fitted with a clamp—it's even better. The Original Clean-A-Fish fillet board system from Intruder has been around for 35 years and it's great for cleaning and preparing panfish, walleye, bass, northern pike, catfish, and members of the salmon family. The base is made of sturdy, fine-grained hardwood that won't dull knives and cleans up easily. The mounted, strong-jawed steel fillet clamp features sharp V-grooves to hold fish securely while leaving both hands free for fish cleaning chores. The 24-inch all-purpose fillet board is sized for cleaning the most popular saltwater and freshwater gamefish. You can also purchase the Intruder Fillet Clamp to

The Original Clean-A-Fish fillet board from Intruder has been around for a long time and is handy for holding fish while filleting. It should be lightly oiled with vegetable oil before use.

fasten to your own board. Wipe down the board with olive or vegetable oil before use, and then occasionally during use to keep water from penetrating the board and also to make the board easy to clean.

Wooden cutting surfaces can also be used for cutting steaks and other cuts, but they are hard to clean once deeply grooved. Synthetic and glass boards are easier.

WORK AREA

Many marinas offer fish-cleaning stations, but many of us fillet or clean our fish at home. This can, of course, be done at the kitchen sink or counter top, but cleaning numbers of fish, especially larger fish is messy at best. An outside work area keeps the mess out of the kitchen, but it still should be easily cleanable. I have an old, stainless steel table set up outside next to my garage. Above the table is an electrical outlet. The outlet is protected by a ground-fault interrupter. Because I often clean fish at night, after a full day of fishing and an hour or so drive home, I've also installed a light with a photocell over the table. When I step up to the work table, the light switches on. Since it's also extremely important to have a means of cleaning up, an outside faucet is located next to the table. I've installed a short piece of discarded hose that reaches the table to make clean up quick and easy.

Portable fish cleaning stations are also available that can be taken to camp with you or used at home. The Pro-Fillet Cleaning System from Bass Pro features an oversized sink with a raised, non-slip cleaning surface with ruler and slotted knife storage, recessed side drains, and built-in slots for 2 x 4 legs (not included). The Pro-Fillet comes with a fillet clamp, sinkhole waste bag clamp, side fillet bag clamp, plus three waste and three fillet storage bags. You can place the unit on a picnic table or add the legs for easy free-standing use.

The Cabela's Fillet Factory Fish Cleaning Table is extremely portable and easy to set up. It comes with a durable polyethylene counter top with 8 x 24-inch cutting board, molded-in fish storage area, knife compartment, bowl holder, ruler, and a unique trash bag holder/drainage system that lets you efficiently eliminate unwanted mess. Sturdy, 18-gauge steel legs are powder coated to prevent rusting and fold flat for storage and transportation. After cleaning your catch, simply remove the trash bag and discard. The high-density

A portable cleaning station such as the Bass Pro Pro-Fillet Cleaning system can be used at campsite or at home. (Photo courtesy Bass Pro.)

polyethylene cutting board and counter top clean up easily with soap and water.

The Bass Pro Bucket Board fits snugly onto any 2-, 4-, 5- or 6-gallon bucket (not included). Lightweight, high density polyethylene, the Bucket Board includes knife storage and a permanent 17-inch ruler. The unit is easily cleaned.

Scalers

Many small panfish are scaled instead of filleted or skinned. A variety of manual fish scalers are available for the chore. Intruder sells a

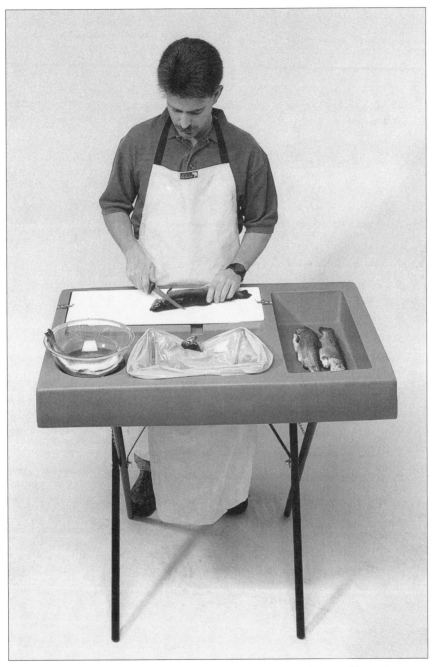

The Cabela's Fillet Factory Fish Cleaning Table is extremely portable and easy to set up. (Photo courtesy Cabela's.)

An even simpler system is the Bass Pro Bucket Board. (Photo courtesy Bass Pro.)

Scalers are often used on small fish, removing the scales but not the skin. The Intruder Scaling Board comes with a clamp and scaler all in one package.

small-size Scaling Board with Clamp and Scaler all in one package. Several mechanical scalers are also available, including one that is pulled behind a boat to scale a whole catch all at one time as you head back to the dock or your home.

OTHER FISH CLEANING TOOLS

For skinning fish, a pair of fish-cleaning pliers is invaluable, especially for cleaning catfish. Bass Pro has two models, including their Deluxe Fish Skinning Pliers that have a sturdy grip and vinyl-coated handles for comfort.

Cabela's carries the Wunder Boner that quickly removes the spine from salmon, trout, char, whitefish, and other salmonoids. To use, simply attach the spine of a cleaned fish to the ring at the end of the stainless steel threaded rod and push the rod through the fish. It's that simple. The rod is marked in one-inch increments allowing you to measure your catch as you go. And, when you're through, the rod breaks down into three pieces that store conveniently in the slots in the base.

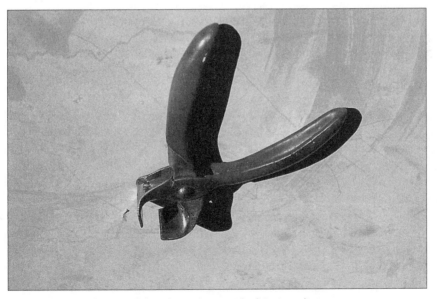

Skinning fish, such as catfish, is best done with skinning pliers.

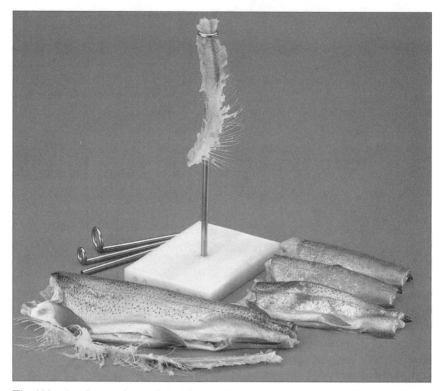

The Wunder Boner from Cabela's quickly and easily removes the spine from trout and salmon. (Photo courtesy Cabela's.)

You'll also need clean cloths, paper towels, clean drinkable water, sealable storage bags, and disposal bags.

United Cutlery has a great Traveling Fisherman's Set that includes a long and short fillet knife, double-edged serrated blade knife, shears, sharpening hone, cleaning glove, tape measure, scales, and even a cutting board, all enclosed in a hard-plastic case.

PRESERVING FISH

Fish can be preserved in several ways, including smoking, pickling, canning, and freezing.

For freezing, a vacuum-packing system such as the Professional II Foodsaver from Tilia provides the best method of preparing fish for the freezer.

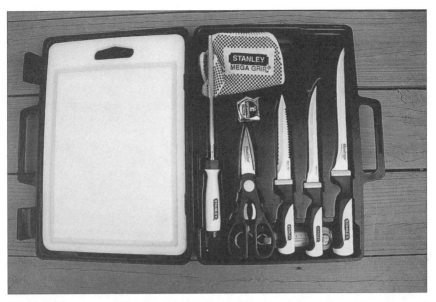

The Traveling Fishermen's Set from United Cutlery includes everything you need for measuring and dressing fish, all in one handy case.

The Professional II FoodSaver from Tilia makes freezing fish easy and provides longer-term storage. (Photo courtesy Tilia.)

Smoking fish is easy with the Bradley Smoker that features a heating element with infinite control and uses special Flavor Bisquettes for smoke.

The Luhr-Jensen Big Chief is an easy-to-use smoker that can hold up to 50 pounds of fish.

For canning you'll need canning jars, lids, rings, and a pressure canner. For pickling, stone jars or plastic tubs.

Smoking fish has been a tradition for generations and is still a very good method of preserving them. A number of manufactured smokers are available, or you can make your own. The Bradley Smoker features an Automatic Smoke Generator, a heating element with infinite control, and an insulated cabinet. The Bradley can cold smoke, hot smoke, and even roast. Its adjustable racks and large capacity help you to handle any smoking project with ease. The

Bradley Smoker automatically produces clean, cool smoke for up to eight hours safely and without supervision by burning patented Flavor Bisquettes rendered from the finest of hardwoods. Maximum cooking temperature is 320 degrees F.

One of the other fish smokers I've tested is the Luhr-Jensen Big Chief. It is a top-loading home electric smokehouse with a 50-pound capacity. The smoker is made of durable, embossed aluminum, and features five easy-slide chrome plated grills. It's vented for proper ventilation and a 450-watt heating element ensures pasteurization. The smoker comes with a bag of Hickory Chips n' Chunks, and a free recipe book. A Trout & Salmon Brine Mix is also available from the company.

Another smoker I've used extensively is the Good-One. A charcoal-fired smoker that is used with wood chunks, the Good-One cold smokes with the fire in one chamber and the meat in another. The heavy-duty metal smoker comes with a thermometer and dampers for controlling the temperature.

The Good-One is a charcoal-fired cold smoker complete with thermometer and control dampers.

Dressing Freshwater Fish

Many species of commonly edible freshwater fish are found in North America. A wide variety of dressing and cleaning techniques can be used, depending on the species, preferred method of cooking, and the tools available.

SCALING

Many fish are scaled, either by rubbing the scales off with a knife, or by using a manual or powered fish scaler. The best fish for scaling include the perches, walleye, and others with tiny, easily removable scales. Scaling fish provides a meat complete with the skin intact. Before scaling, the fish should be washed in clean water. Remove the scales by scraping the fish, beginning at the tail and moving toward the head. A dull knife, the edge of a spoon, or special scaling tools can be used. Several powered scaling tools are also available that make the chore even easier. As you can guess, scaling is best done outside, rather than on the kitchen table.

FILLETING

One of the most popular methods of cleaning many fish species is filleting. Filleting provides, in most instances, a boneless piece of meat called a fillet. Fillets can be skinless or have the skin left on. Fillets can be pan fried, deep fried, poached, grilled, or smoked. Some fish are best filleted, including many freshwater and saltwater species. Others are best steaked. Much depends on the method to be used in cooking, as well as the species. Even catfish, often

Numerous freshwater fish, from small to huge, offer fishing fun and great food for the table.

Small fish are quite often simply scaled, scraping off the scales but leaving the skin on.

steaked, can be filleted. Although I often dress tiny bluegill and crappie in another method, the larger bluegill and crappie are delicious filleted.

Whether using a manual or electric-powered fillet knife, I like to hold the knife in one hand (in this case my left, since I'm left-handed), and grasp the fish with the other. This keeps the hand holding the knife clean and free of blood and slime. A board with a clamp can make the chore easier, or you can simply hold the fish by the lower jaw with one hand and fillet with the other. A sharp knife and smooth flat surface to fillet are musts. You don't have to get fancy, however. I've used the back of a boat or canoe paddle in many instances.

Small Fish Fillets

Make the first cut just behind the gills. Many simply slice straight down to the backbone with this cut, but I prefer to first slice in under the gills and toward the head, then turn the blade back toward the tail. This provides more meat on smaller fish. On bluegills

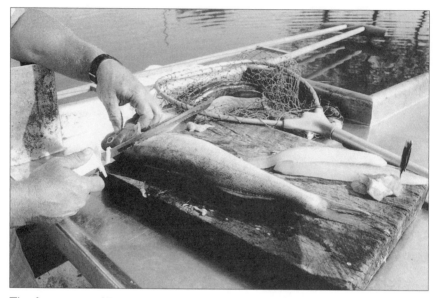

The first step in filleting a fish is to cut down to its backbone just behind the gills.

On small to medium sized fish, turn the knife blade and slice toward the tail, cutting through the rib bones and allowing the blade to follow the backbone.

To remove the skin, stop the cut just before the tail, leaving a skin "hinge." Flop the fillet over, skin side down, and slice between the skin and meat.

If the skin is to be left on as with this salmon, continue the cut to the tail to remove the fillet with skin.

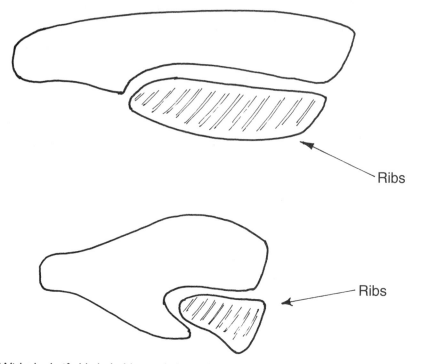

With the knife blade held at a slight angle, cut away the ribs and belly to leave a boneless fillet.

you have to lift the flap behind the gill to get the blade in place. Next, turn the knife blade and cut along the backbone, through the ribs, to the tail. If the fillet is to be left with the skin on, as in the case of salmon, continue the cut through the skin at the tail.

If you prefer skinless fillets, stop the cut just before you reach the tail. Using the fillet knife, flop the fillet back exposing the meat and, with the fillet lying skin-side-down on the cutting board, slide the knife under the meat at the tail, between the meat and the skin, and slice back toward the front part of the fillet to separate the meat and skin. With a manual fillet knife a sawing motion will make the cut easier. Sometimes you'll make a mishap and slice too close to the tail to provide enough skin to hold the fillet to the carcass to complete the cut. In this case, you'll have to first make a cut between the skin and meat and hold the fillet down by the skin with the skin facing down on the cutting board and make the slice. After you've experienced this problem a time or two, you'll be very careful not to allow it to happen again.

Turn the fish over and repeat the filleting and skinning steps for the opposite side.

The fillet will still have the rib bones in place. With the fillet lying flesh side up, insert the fillet knife next to the rib bones and slice the ribs and belly section away. Make sure you do not leave bones in the fillet (they're usually boneless). On fish such as crappie, bluegill, and bass, you can increase the amount of meat in the fillet by making a V-cut in the bottom of the belly since there are no bones located in this area.

Larger Fish Fillets

Large bass, salmon, and other fish with heavy rib bones are best filleted by cutting around the rib bones and leaving them intact on the backbone. Begin the cut just behind the gills and pectoral fins, cutting down to the backbone. Then make a cut along the dorsal fin, cutting parallel to the side of the fish and only until you feel

To fillet larger fish, make the initial cut just behind the gills down to the backbone.

Make a cut along the dorsal fin and top along the backbone but just to the ribs.

the blade hitting the ribs. Continue this cut, using short strokes, and lift up the flap of meat as you work around the rib cage. This cut will extend about three-quarters of the length of the fish or until you no longer feel the rib cage. Once you are free of it, position your blade parallel to the backbone and continue the cut toward the tail.

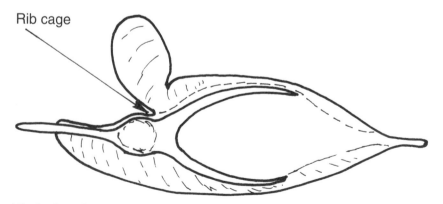

Lift the flap of meat and cut around the ribcage until you pass the ribcage.

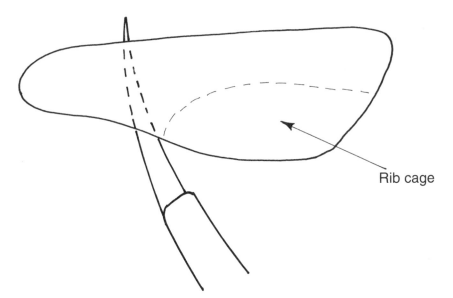

Once free of the ribcage, continue the cut along the backbone toward the tail.

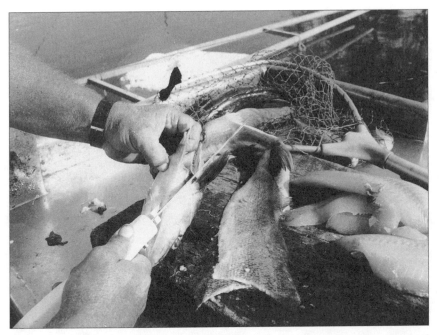

To remove cheek and throat meat, after filleting, slice from the throat toward the underside of the jaw.

Repeat the slice on the opposite side of the throat.

Cut off the fins.

Skin out the piece of meat.

The resulting boneless piece of meat.

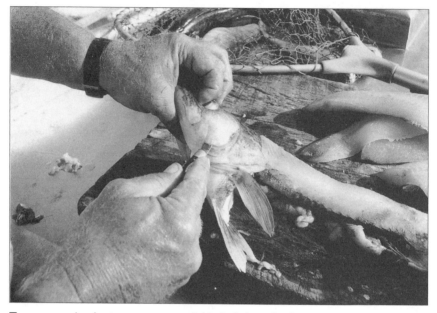

To remove cheek pieces use a small-bladed sharp knife to gouge the meat from the skull.

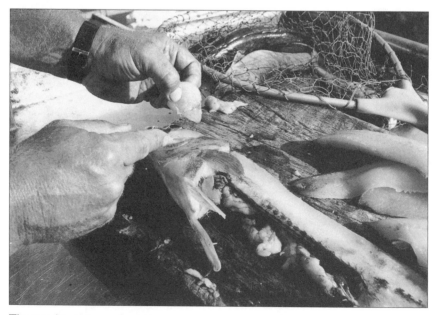

The resulting piece of meat.

As you reach the tail, leave the fillet attached. Flop the fillet back off the carcass and cut through the meat down to the skin but not through it at the tail. Then turn the fillet knife flat down on the skin and work surface and cut the fillet from the skin, working from the tail cut toward the front of the fillet. Hold the fish by the head with your opposite hand or use a board with a clamp. A sawing motion will make the chore easier if you're using a manual knife. This cut is extremely easy with an electric fillet knife. Turn the fish over and repeat the filleting and skinning steps for the opposite side.

Many fish have "cheek" meat. On larger fish, such as walleye, it's not only delicious but a fairly large piece of meat that many people don't know about or ignore. Simply slice into the cheek and gouge out the chunk of meat.

Butterfly Fillets

Fish such as bass or walleye can be filleted in the butterfly method, which provides a double piece of meat that can be stuffed and baked. Two methods can be used. In both methods the fish is first scaled, but not skinned.

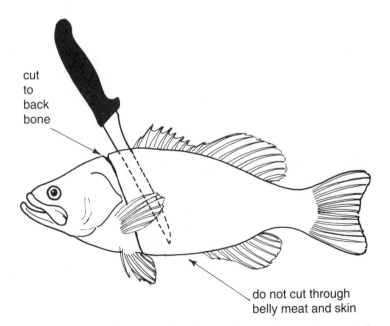

cut
to
back
bone

do not cut through
belly meat and skin

To butterfly fillet a fish, first scale, but do not skin it. Next, make a cut along the backbone in the usual manner, but do not cut through the belly skin.

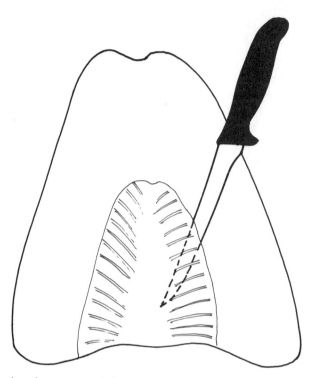

Cut away the ribs, or around them.

The first method is to make a fillet starting along the backbone in the normal manner, but do not cut through the belly skin. Next, turn the fish over and remove the fillet from the opposite side. Spread the double fillet out, skin side down and slice away the ribs.

On larger fish, another method is to cut down alongside the backbone to the top of the rib cage. Carefully work around the rib cage but do not cut through the belly skin. Repeat on the opposite side. Cut through the backbone at the tail and head and lift out the backbone, ribs, and entrails. This actually produces a fish with head and tail in place ready for stuffing for your more elaborate baked dishes.

NORTHERN PIKE

Northern pike are usually cut into two fillets, with the skin left on. Northern Pike have a row of "Y bones" that should be removed dur-

Northern pike and muskellunge are dressed somewhat differently because of the row of Y bones along their sides.

ing the dressing steps. The first step is to remove the two anal fins (those located just behind the belly). Next, fillet the sides from the carcass, again leaving the skin on the fillets. Two methods can be used for removing the Y bones.

The first method is used on small pike and leaves the fillet intact, but with bones removed. With the flesh side up, insert the fillet knife at an angle along the lateral line. You can locate the Y bones with your fingers and they'll also be visible. Slice along the top side of the bones, feeling for where they curve back under, and follow with the knife. Then turn the knife and go below the lateral line and slice at an angle to meet the first cut. Remove the Y-bone section, and then remove the skin.

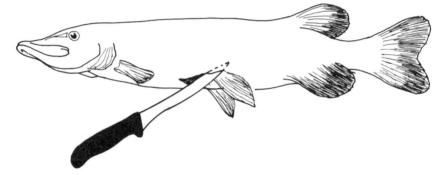

Remove the two anal fins.

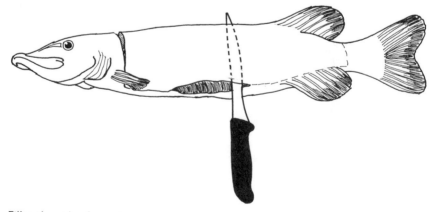

Fillet the sides from the carcass.

cut

cut

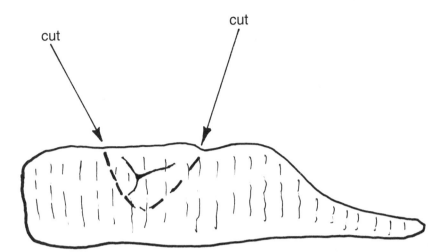

On small pike, remove the skin and slice under the Y bones at an angle to re-move them.

On larger pike, it's best to first fillet the carcass but leave the skin on. Then chunk up the carcass into more manageable pieces. Because the tail section does not have the Y bones, it is first re-moved from the skin by cutting straight down to, but not through, the skin. Then slice between the skin and meat to the tail. Remove the skin from the rest of the fillet. Next, remove the rib cage and belly. Cut the remainder of the carcass into pieces approximately three inches long. Again look for and feel for the Y bones, which protrude somewhat. On large pike you can cut straight down on the top edge of the Y bones and remove the top loin section by itself. Then cut from the bottom side of the Y bones, turn, and follow them to remove them from the bottom piece of meat.

Another tactic with Northern pike is to cut separate fillets from the fish, leaving the Y bones on the carcass. The first step is to re-move the top loin section. Grasp the fish by its head and position it on its belly. Cut straight down just behind the head to the back-bone. Next, turn the knife and cut along the top of the backbone to the beginning of the front fin near the tail. Turn the knife back up and cut away this boneless section.

This exposes the backbone and the Y bones. Position the fish on its side with the backbone facing you. Begin cutting about a quarter inch deep on the outer edge of the Y bones, cutting to the

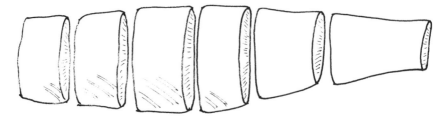

On large pike, leave the skin on but cut into manageable chunks, including the tail section. Remove the skin from the tail section. Cut the top loin section above the Y bones from the fillet. Cut the Y bones from the sides.

rear of the fish and stopping at the point where the first fillet was removed. Beginning behind the head and the back dorsal fin, cut directly down to the spine. Lift the flap of boneless meat and continue cutting lengthwise along the outside of the Y bones. Continue slicing along the outside of the ribs, holding the flap of meat up with your fingers as you make the cut. Cut through the belly skin to meet the prior cut and remove the boneless fillet. Repeat for the opposite side.

The next step is to cut off the two fillets on either side of the tail piece. These do not have Y bones. Slide the knife along the backbone to remove the fillet, then turn the fish over and repeat for the opposite side. This provides five boneless fillets. The final step is to

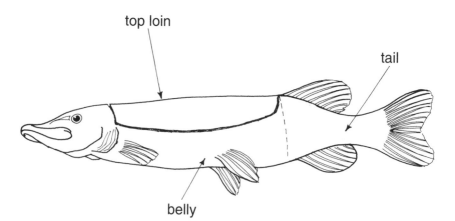

You can also dress to leave the Y bones on the carcass. Cut away the top loin section, stopping at the beginning of the front fin near the tail. Cut around the Y bones and ribcage. Remove the tail fillets and skin all pieces.

cut the skin away from each piece. In order to remove any "fishy" taste, you should also cut away the red meat.

DRESSING PANFISH

I prefer to dress small panfish, such as bluegill or perch, in a different manner, removing the fins, intestines, tail, and skin. This method provides a whole, but small, fish that is perfect for pan or deep-fat frying. I have a couple of friends who prefer to leave the tail in place, especially for deep frying.

Position the fish upright on its belly, or lay the fish on its side. I prefer the upright method. Slice down just behind the head to remove it completely. Position the fish on one side and, with a small fillet knife, cut along both sides of the anal and dorsal fins. Make the cut from the head cut to the tail, but don't cut too deeply. Repeat for the opposite side.

Starting at the top and near the tail, grasp the dorsal fin with fish-dressing pliers and pull back towards the head. The fins will come out in one piece. Next, grasp the anal fin near the tail and pull this out as well. This step should remove the fins and intestines all in one move. If it doesn't, use your finger to scrape out the intestines.

At the top, near the head, is a small flap of loose skin. Holding the fish down with one hand, grasp the skin with the fish dressing

Small panfish such as bluegill or perch are often dressed leaving the bones in.

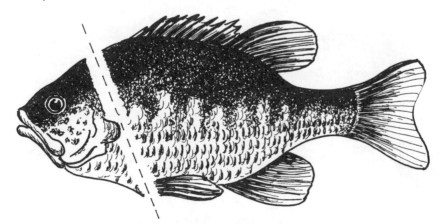

Stand fish upright on its belly and cut off the head just behind the gills.

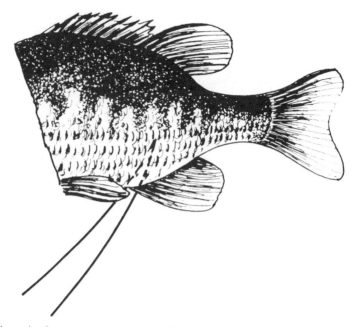

Use sharp knife to cut along both sides of anal and dorsal fins. Continue cut along belly.

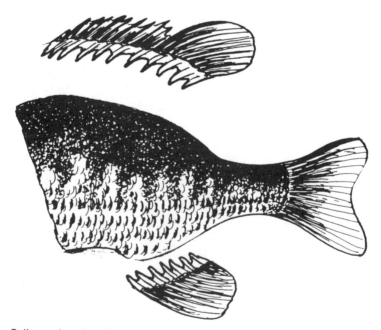

Pull out dorsal and anal fins with a pair of fish-cleaning pliers. Entrails will come out with anal fins.

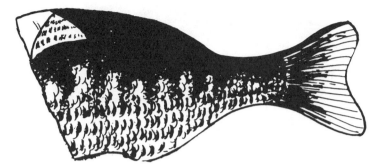

Grasp flap of skin at top of shoulder and peel off. Repeat for opposite side.

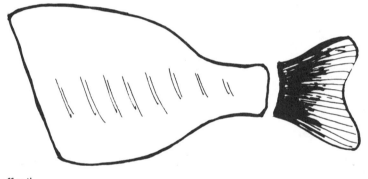

Cut off tail.

pliers at that point and peel the skin off. Repeat for the opposite side. The last step is to cut off the tail or leave if desired.

CLEANING TROUT

Trout are often simply gutted, leaving the head, skin, tail, and fins in place. This can be done at home or in camp, but is often done right at streamside. One reason is trout are a cold-water species and the flesh tends to deteriorate rapidly after the fish dies. Cleaning trout is quick and simple and, with a little practice, you can do it in less than a minute. All that's needed is a sharp knife.

The first step is to make a cut from the anal opening up to the gills. Make a straight line cut. You don't have to cut deeply, just through the belly skin and muscle. Stop the cut before you reach

Make a cut from the anal opening to the gills. Trout are often cleaned stream-side, eviscerating but leaving them whole otherwise.

Place your finger in the fish's mouth and press on the tongue to extend the V-shaped "tab" of the lower jaw. Slice through the tab at the top.

Grasp the tab and pull down to remove entrails.

Use your fingernail to scrape away the blood sac.

the V-shaped area just below the bottom jaw. Place your finger inside the fish's mouth and press on the tongue. This will extend the V-shaped portion of its lower jaw. Slice through the tab at the top.

Holding the fish by the lower jaw in one hand, grasp the V tab and pull down. This will remove the gills and entrails all in one motion.

Holding the trout in one hand, use a fingernail of the opposite hand to run along the entire backbone to break and remove the blood sac. Wipe the fish off with clean paper towels, or wash in water. The least amount of water contact results in firmer flesh.

CATFISH

Catfish can be dressed in several ways, depending on the size of the fish and the intended method of cooking. Catfish tend to be slimy and hard to hold. A good Kevlar skinning glove can make the chore easier; so can a fish board with a clamp.

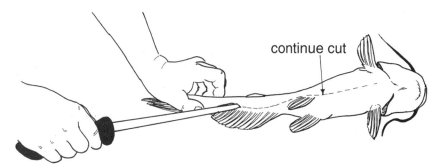

Make a cut on each side of the anal fins. Continue the belly cut up from the tail to just behind the gills.

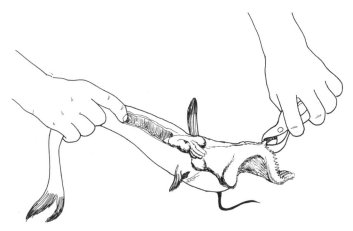

Using a pair of fish pliers, peel out the anal fin and entrails.

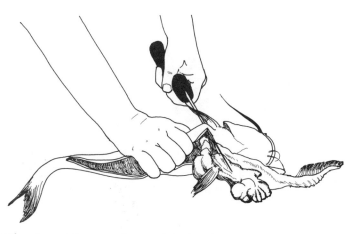

Peel out the dorsal fin, cut off around the head, and remove it.

Catfish can be filleted or skinned.

Small Catfish

On small cats I like to dress roughly in the same manner as for small panfish, except the head is left on during the initial steps. The first step is to insert a knife blade and slice along both sides of both anal and dorsal fins from just behind the head to the tail.

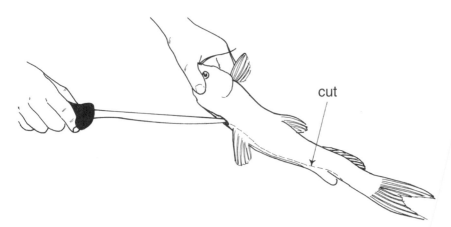

cut

To skin small cats, the first step is to cut along the back from the head to the ta on both sides of the dorsal fin.

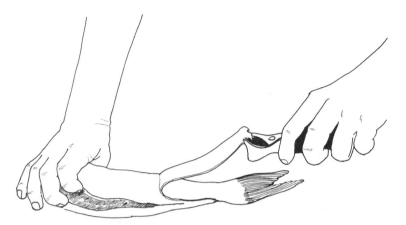

Use fish-cleaning pliers to peel off the skin.

Holding the fish by the tail, use a pair of fish-skinning pliers to peel the anal fins out. The intestines will also come when peeling out the anal fins.

Remove the head by first cutting through the muscle of the back, sides, and belly. Then twist off the head. Grasp the dorsal fins with the fish pliers and pull them out.

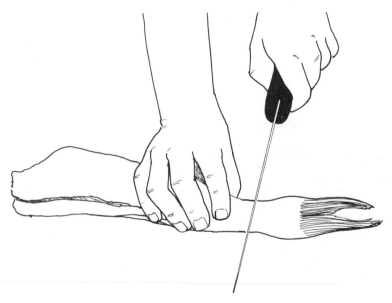

Cut off the tail.

Grip the skin at the top of the shoulders with the fish-skinning pliers and peel back towards the tail. Repeat for the opposite side. Finally, cut off the tail.

Large Catfish

On larger cats the skin is often hard to peel off. It's easier to leave the head on the cat until the last step, providing a better "hand-hold."

The first step is to cut through the skin behind the head and all around the fish. Then make the cuts on either side of the dorsal and anal fins, from behind the head to the tail.

Hold the catfish by the head with one hand and grasp the skin with a pair of fish-dressing pliers. Peel the skin off toward the tail. Peel the skin off the opposite side.

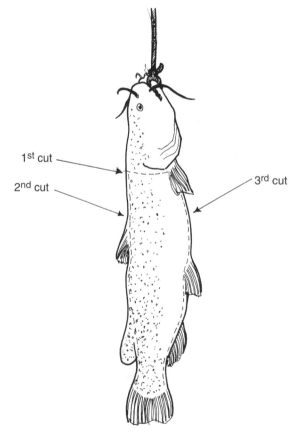

1st cut

2nd cut

3rd cut

To skin a really big catfish, hang it by a rope from a sturdy tree limb. Make cuts through the skin just behind the head and down the top of the back and belly on both sides of the anal and dorsal fins. Using fish-skinning pliers, peel the skin down off the sides to the tail.

Cut through the gullet. Next, cut down the belly, being careful not to cut into the intestines. Pull out the anal fin and intestines.

Grasp the dorsal fin at the back edge with pliers and pull it forward towards the head. After breaking the dorsal fin out away from the backbone, cut completely around the head. Bend the head backwards to snap the backbone, and cut to remove it.

Holding the fish by the tail, grasp the anal fin at the back edge and peel it out, away and towards the head cut. The last step is to cut off the tail. Large catfish that have been skinned whole can be cooked whole or, if it's a really large cat, can be cut crosswise into steaks. On large fish it's a good idea to cut off the belly flesh. This area tends to hold the most fat, carries the most contaminants, and also has more of the "off flavors."

It's also important to remove any red-line or lateral tissue from catfish. Flathead catfish tend to have more of this than the other cats.

For extremely large cats the best tactic is to hang the cat up by the head with a rope. Then make the cuts to remove the fins, intestines,

Grasp the dorsal fin, bend it back toward the head until it breaks free of the backbone, and remove it.

cut

bend
back

Cut around the head and twist the carcass from the head. Cut off the tail.

and skin. The carcass can then be removed from the head by cutting around the head and twisting the two in opposite directions.

Catfish Fillets

Small- to medium-sized catfish can also be filleted. For small cats, fillet with the rib cage in, then cut away the rib cage. For larger cats you may prefer to cut around the rib cage as described for filleting other large fish. In both cases the belly meat and fat should also be removed. Large fillets can be baked whole or cut into smaller chunks for frying.

STEAKING AND CHUNKING OTHER FISH

Salmon and large trout can also be cut into steaks, leaving the skin in place. The first step is to cut the belly open and remove the intestines, anal fins, and blood sac. Next, make a cut on either side of the dorsal fin and peel it out of the carcass. Position the fish up on its belly and, using a sharp knife, cut just behind the head to remove it. To create steaks continue cutting at right angles to the

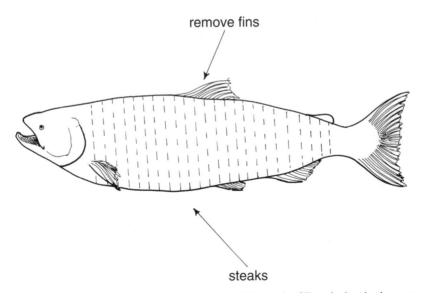

Large fish such as salmon, large trout, and catfish can be filleted, chunked, or cut into steaks.

backbone of the fish, cutting the steaks three-quarters- to one-inch thick. It may take a good deal of pressure to cut the backbone on some larger fish. Cut away the belly fat from the steaks. To chunk for broiling or baking, cut into two-inch thick portions.

PADDLEFISH

Paddlefish or spoonbill, which can weigh upward of 160 pounds, offer some of the best of "big game" angling. Their meat is moist and delicious and can be fried or smoked. When fried it tastes like channel catfish. The roe from spoonbill is often substituted for

cut

To clean paddlefish, hang from a sturdy tree limb by the paddle and cut around the base of the tail. Pull down on the tail to remove the cartilage notochord.

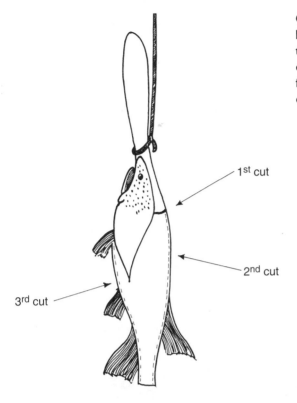

Cut through the skin behind the head and peel the skin down using fish-dressing pliers. Gut the fish, remove the head, and cut away all red meat.

1st cut

2nd cut

3rd cut

caviar and it can be salted and dried in that manner, or it can be fried in butter and served on toast.

Paddlefish, like sharks, have a cartilage rather than a bone skeleton. They also do not have scales. Paddlefish can be skinned and gutted or filleted. Due to the composition of their skeleton, however, a different method is often used. The fish is hung by its paddle and a cut is made in the skin around the tail. With a helper holding the carcass securely, you can twist the tail sharply and then pull the tail down to pull out the notochord (the spinelike structure that supports the axis of the paddlefish's body).

Cut through the skin just behind the head and peel the skin down using pliers. Remove the head and gut the fish. The carcass can then be cut into steaks or fillets. Expert spoonbillers suggest trimming off all red meat and using only the white inner flesh.

If the fish is to be smoked, cut the carcass in half lengthwise. Paddlefish can also be grilled. When smoking or grilling, leave the skin on the fish.

CARP AND OTHER ROUGH FISH

The "rough" fishes include carp, buffalo, freshwater drum (sheepshead), burbot (or lawyer or eelpout), bowfin (dogfish), suckers, quillback or white carp, and gar. The name comes from the fact that most are not gamefish; some are commercially fished and in many cases most of these species are considered "undesirable," primarily in the United States. In other countries many of these same fish are consid-

Carp, buffalo, suckers, and other species considered "rough" fish in America are considered delicacies in Europe.

ered gourmet foods. Many of these so-called rough fish are delicious and are underutilized both by sport anglers and as food for the table. When I was a kid back in the 1940s fish sellers came around the countryside selling carp and buffalo and one of my father's favorite pastimes was angling for these fish. They were a common food in our household and we enjoyed them deep fried as well as canned.

Rough fish can be baked whole, smoked, pickled, canned, steamed, deep fried, pan fried, or used in chowders. The method of cooking, and the species, dictates the method of dressing. In many instances, special dressing and cooking techniques are required to get the best taste. Most of these fish also have numerous bones with which you must contend as well. Some species, since they are primarily bottom feeders, can also acquire a musty taste, especially during the hot summer months when excessive growths of algae may be present in the calm backwaters that many of these species frequent.

Carp

Carp were first imported from Europe to the United States in the 1880s. Izaak Walton called them, "the queen of rivers, a stateless, good and very subtle fish." In Europe and Asia, carp is considered a delicacy. These days carp can be found in waters throughout the United States. The flesh can be excellent, but consists of many tiny Y bones, one reason many cooks avoid it.

Suckers

Buffalo are members of the sucker family and include the bigmouth, smallmouth, and black. These are the largest of the sucker clan and can reach weights of over 80 pounds. They were once a very important commercial fish. Their flesh is delicious, with a fine white texture, but also has the Y bones. Other, smaller suckers include the carpsuckers, hogsucker, redhorse, blue, and white suckers. Their flesh is also white and very tasty, but with the numerous Y bones.

Freshwater Drum

Also called white perch, sheepshead, rock perch, or croaker, drum can attain weights of over 30 pounds. The flesh is white and firm, and does not contain the small bones. Found throughout much of the United States, freshwater drum is a very underutilized food fish.

Dressing and Cleaning

In most instances, these rough fish species are "fleeced," which is a method of scaling. A long thin sharp fillet knife is inserted just in front of the tail and facing toward the head. A sawing motion is then used to "fleece" the scales from the skin. Loosen the scales at the tail first, then the belly and finally along the sides. Done properly, the entire mass of scales can then be lifted from the skin. The fleeced skin appears pearly white and smooth. Carp and other rough fish can also be skinned if preferred, and skinning does tend to take more of the "off" flavor away.

If the fish is to be baked, remove the head, fins, and entrails. The fish is usually left whole, otherwise, so a bread stuffing can be placed in the body cavity. Smoking is a popular method of preserving carp, and if the fish is to be smoked it can be cut into steaks, or cross sections. You can also saw the entire length of the backbone to divide the fish into two halves. The cleaned fish can also be filleted after fleecing, when you want to retain the skin for pickling or canning. Carp and other rough fish can also be filleted in the man-

Most rough fish are "fleeced," a method of removing scales and the light membrane beneath them.

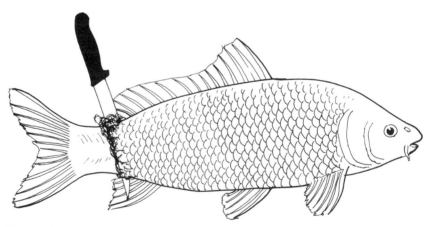

With a sharp knife, use a sawing motion under the scales from the tail toward the head.

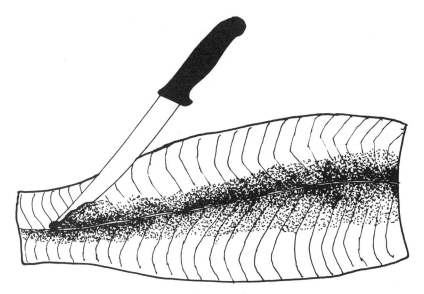

Remove the head, tail, and entrails. Cut all red meat.

ner of other fish.

One of the problems with carp and other rough fish is a musty taste they may develop in certain waters during hot weather. This taste is primarily located in the skin as well as the red streak along the lateral line of the sides. It's best to remove this dark red streak along with the "mud vein" just under the dark meat area.

Suckers, including redhorse, carp, buffalo, and quillback (white or emur carp) have numerous small Y bones located throughout the flesh. These are tiny bones free-floating on each side of the body in rows. The bones are not connected to the rest of the skeleton. For most recipes these bones must be reduced in some manner.

These species can be deep fried and are delicious, but the small bones must first be "scored." After fleecing or skinning, and/or filleting, the flesh should be scored every ¼ inch, cutting through the Y bones. Don't cut entirely through the fillet, only down to below the bones. This takes a bit of practice, but you'll soon be able to feel when you reach the bone-free area. The bones are actually located only in the upper one third of the meat.

In the case of whole fish rather than fillets, make sure the scoring cuts are down to the backbone. When the fish is deep fried, the cooking oils penetrate the bones, softening them and leaving them

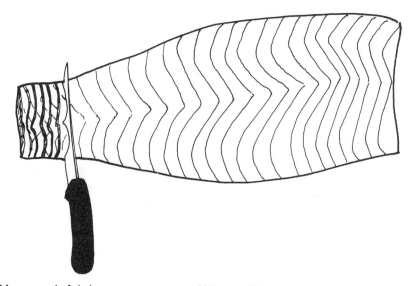

Most rough fish have numerous tiny Y bones. These must be scored through about every ¼ inch, down to the backbone on whole fish, and just through the bones on fillets.

undetectable. These fish can also be filleted, and the fillets frozen, and then run through a food grinder twice to break down the Y bones. The ground meat can then be used in hash, sausage, or patties.

Dogfish

Dogfish are also often called bowfin. These are a living fossil featuring a reptilian head and a bow-shaped tail. The flesh is white, but somewhat soft. The most common use is as a smoked fish. They are normally skinned and chunked.

Burbot

Also called "lawyer" fish or eelpout, these fish are the only member of the cod family that is found in fresh water. The flesh is extremely white, quite tasty and without the Y bones. Burbot are normally skinned, and this must be done as soon as they are caught because the meat deteriorates quite rapidly. They're also called "poor man's lobster" since they taste superb boiled, but they can also be pan-fried.

Gar

Another living fossil, the gar species includes the longnose, spotted (shortnose), and alligator. Gar are primarily found in quiet, warm backwaters or turbid rivers. The meat is boneless, white, and has an excellent flavor all its own. There's even a gar association, G.A.S.S. (Gar Angler's Sportsman's Society). The association has a Web site with information about the fish along with a number of recipes. The most common method of cooking is by deep frying. The eggs, how-ever, are poisonous and should not be eaten.

Cleaning gar is not particularly easy, especially the larger fish. The following information on cleaning gar comes from my good friend Keith "Catfish" Sutton, author of *Catfish's Cookbook*. "The first step is to cut off its head and tail with a hatchet. Then use tin snips to split the bony hide along the fish's length, then peel the meat from the armored hull and fillet the meat from along the length of the backbone as you might cut a tenderloin off a deer." Keith warns to wear gloves, such as Kevlar fish cleaning gloves to protect your hands while cutting the bony hide and removing the meat. The edges of the hide can cut like glass. Cut the loins into smaller pieces for frying.

Gar offer a greatly overlooked and tasty white meat. Some gar can attain great size. *Photo courtesy of Muzzy Products Corporation.*

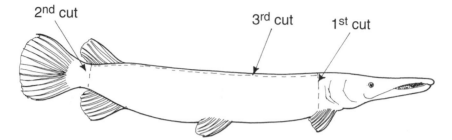

Cut off the head and tail. Next, wearing Kevlar fish-cleaning gloves, use tin snips to cut through the bony hide along the top of the fish's length.

Cut off the top loin section along the top of the backbone.

Dressing Saltwater Fish and Shellfish

For the most part, many saltwater finfish are dressed in the same manner as freshwater fish. Some species, however, are dressed differently, due to their body makeup, or simply because of their size.

Small fish may be scaled, eviscerated, and headed. Or they may be skinned, eviscerated, and left whole or filleted. Medium-size fish are often scaled or skinned, eviscerated, and then left whole for baking, or they can also be filleted. Larger fish are normally skinned and filleted or steaked, or, in some cases, the skin is left on. The fish may also first be planked, and then steaked.

TUNA

Great care must be taken with tuna to assure quality meat. Tuna are great fighters, even when landed on board, and the first steps are to protect excessive thrashing of the fish and to keep handling to a minimum. Don't throw or drop the fish on board. Gaff the tuna in the lower jaw if possible, then bring the fish carefully aboard and place it gently on a rubber mat or piece of old carpet. Immediately stun the fish by striking it on the head with a club. Driving a spike into the brain behind the eyes, and holding your hands firmly over its eyes helps to minimize thrashing.

The tuna must then be bled and gutted. Lift up each pectoral fin and make a cut just behind the fin. This allows the major artery to drain. Make another cut on the caudal peduncle below the second and third finlet from the tail.

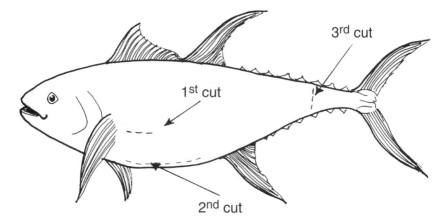

Tuna must be stunned and bled as soon as caught.

To gut, make a cut from the pectoral fin to the anal fin. This cut should be made fairly shallow to prevent cutting into the entrails, which could release bile and stomach materials into the body cavity. Carefully remove all entrails and organs.

Submerge the carcass in an ice and seawater slurry consisting of two parts ice to one part sea water. Agitating the slurry will help prevent warm water pockets and lower the temperature of the carcass more quickly.

Fresh tuna can be eaten fresh or canned. Fresh tuna is great smoked, grilled, or blackened. It can also be broiled and used in

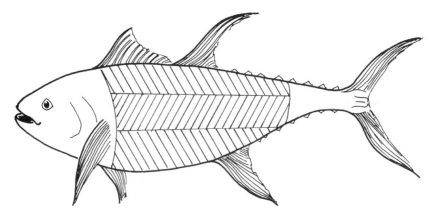

Depending on the size, the fish may be steaked or portions planked, cut into fillets—even sushi or sashimi.

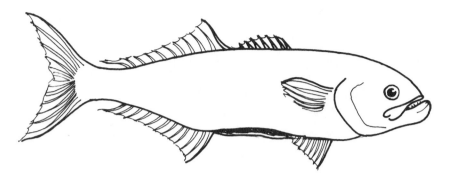

Whole, gutted.

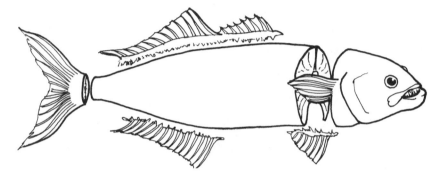

Headed, gutted, de-finned.

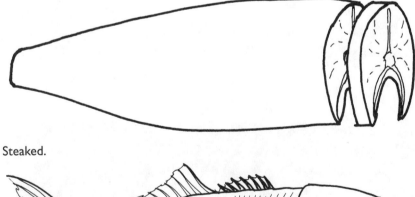

Steaked.

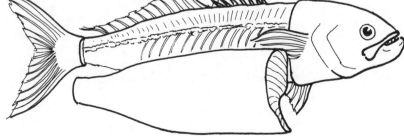

Filleted.

Saltwater finfish offer great sport as well as great-tasting food.

Filleting is a common method of preparing finfish. To begin filleting, make a cut behind the gills, down to the backbone.

Cut along the backbone only to the ribcage.

Cut down to the backbone around the top of the ribcage.

Peel out the fillet, cutting away as needed.

Remove skin from the fillet.

Cut away any red meat from the outside of the fillet.

cold salads and casseroles. Tuna can also be canned if you have the proper equipment.

Small tuna can be filleted or gutted and broiled whole. Larger tuna are usually planked or filleted, and then cut into steaks. Tuna steaks can be cut from the entire carcass. The best meat from the larger tuna is found in the shoulder or loin area.

Tuna is also served raw, as either sushi, which is thin slices served on rice, or sashimi, which is thin, bite-sized pieces. Since tuna fat is prized because it adds flavor, the belly flaps, with its higher concentrations of fat are considered premium or sashimi-grade.

The first step in preparing tuna for sushi is to cut off the tail and head. Next, fillet each side from the spine. Cut these fillets lengthwise into three strips. The back or upper strips and lower or belly strips are triangular in cross section. These triangular strips are then sliced into thin pieces.

The risk of becoming infected with a marine parasite from eating raw tuna is fairly low and most parasites cause only slight to moderate illness. The F.D.A., however, recommends that before eating raw, marinated, or partially cooked fish, it should be frozen to −20 degrees C (−4 degrees F.) or below for seven days in a freezer.

SHARK

Shark meat is excellent, but must be handled carefully to prevent spoilage. Sharks have as much as 2.5 percent urea in their blood and if the blood is not drained immediately from the shark, the urea quickly deteriorates into ammonia. This produces the dry taste and "sharky" odor of improperly handled shark meat.

The first step is to immobilize the shark with a club. Gut the shark immediately. The carcass should then be washed and cleaned to remove as much blood as possible. It's important, however, not to discard the offal in the water because it can cause shark fishing in the area to turn off. The gutted shark is then placed into a saltwater-ice slush. Ice alone will not suffice. It is important to keep the shark meat below 40 degrees F. If temperatures are allowed to get above 40 degrees, bacterial growth in the meat can skyrocket.

Back at the dock, the shark is skinned. Cut all the way around, just through the skin behind the head. Next, make a cut along the backbone from the head cut to the tail. Make a cut along the belly

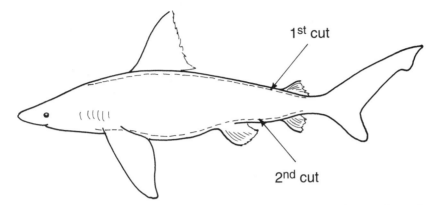

Gut sharks as soon as possible. Back at the dock, cut along the top from the head to the tail. If the shark hasn't been gutted, cut along the belly in the same manner, and eviscerate.

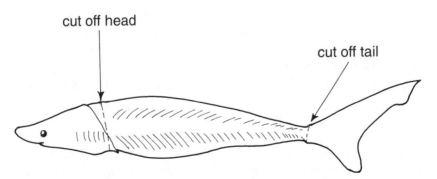

Peel off the skin using pliers and a sharp knife to assist.

Cut off head and tail; remove all dark red meat from the sides. The carcass can be filleted or steaked.

in the same manner. Then, using fish pliers and a sharp knife, skin out the carcass. Shark skin is tough and it usually takes some pulling and judicious cutting to remove it completely.

Next, cut off the head and tail. You must also remove the heavy bloodline or dark red meat along the sides of the shark. Then, cut the shark into fillets.

Some shark experts prefer to cut off the fins, head, and caudal or tail fin immediately after catching. This makes it easier to fit larger sharks into the fish box and also provides for better bleeding. Some anglers also do not skin the shark, but simply slice it into steaks about one inch thick.

At home, wash the meat thoroughly before freezing or preparing it for cooking. You can further remove any residual ammonia from the meat by soaking the fillets in lemon juice before freezing or cooking.

If the shark is fairly large you may wish to keep the valuable skin. In that case, the skin is fleshed, salted, rolled, and/or frozen until it can be tanned.

FLOUNDER

A wide variety of flat fishes are available, ranging in size from tiny to the huge halibut, and they're all delicious. The smaller flat fishes are often cooked whole. Simply eat around the numerous bones. Small- and medium-sized flat fishes are usually filleted, while the huge halibuts are planked, then steaked like other large fish.

Filleting flat fish is somewhat different than other fishes because of the bone structure. The meat is actually all on the topside and that's where the fillet comes from. The first step is to place the flat fish on a cutting board, eyes up, and cut down to the bones just behind the head. Insert the fillet knife behind the pelvic bone, and slice from the head toward the tail, pushing the knife blade just into the backbone. Use your hand to lift the skin and meat up and away from the bones. Turn the fish around and repeat on the opposite side. Pull the loosened skin and flesh pieces upward and cut away from the backbone.

You can also fillet the two sides separately, simply cutting down on either side of the backbone. Skin the fillet or fillets by holding the tail down with a clamp and slicing between the skin and flesh with a thin, sharp fillet knife.

For stuffed sole, the flat fish is scaled and then filleted, leaving the skin on. The two sides of the fillet are then folded over the stuff-

Small flatfishes are often filleted, but somewhat differently due to their configuration.

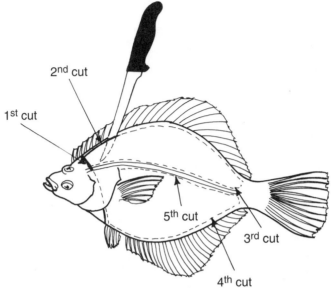

Two fillets can be removed from the top side by cutting along the backbone to the pelvic bone.

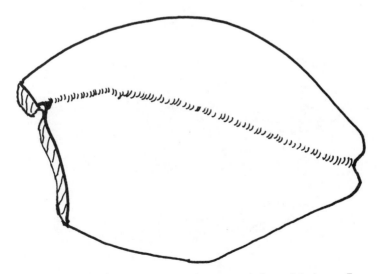

The fillets can also be kept as one, cutting around the pelvic bone. For stuffed sole, leave the skin on and pin the fillets together around the stuffing.

ing and pinned together. Meat can be cut away from the front of the fillet, leaving a flap of skin to help hold the stuffing in place.

SKATES AND RAYS

Some of the most underutilized saltwater species are the skates and rays. Prepared properly, they have much the same flavor as scallops. Like sharks, however, they must be bled and iced immediately after catching to prevent the meat from souring. Some species of rays also have barbed stingers on the tail. Cutting off the tail above the stinger not only prevents danger from the stinger but also aids in bleeding out the ray.

It's best to dress the ray within 15 to 20 minutes after it has been caught to prevent the rapid deteoriation caused by urea. The wings are the most usable portions of the skate or ray, although larger rays can provide a fairly large back or loin section of meat. Simply cut off the wings and wash thoroughly to remove any blood. Then cut away the thin outer edge of the wing. Slice the wing into thin strips

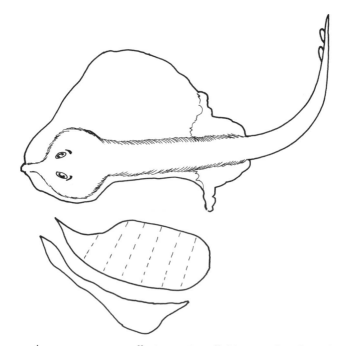

To prepare skates or rays, cut off wings, trim off thin outside edges, skin out, and cut into thin strips.

Skin out the strips.

and remove the skin from the strips. You can also skin out the wings on larger rays, and then cut the meat into strips for frying. You can also boil or poach the wings with the skin on. The skin comes off quite easily after boiling.

Marinating the wings in a brine or acidic solution should be done to remove any excess urea. Lemon juice is often used if the skate is to be broiled, while milk soaking is recommended when the skate is to be deep-fried. You can also soak in a brine mixture of one cup of salt or one-half cup of white vinegar in a gallon of water. Soak in the vinegar solution for four hours and four to eight hours in the saltwater brine solution. After soaking, scrape the skin with a knife blade and rinse.

Rays and skates should not be overcooked because they become extremely dry. They can be boiled, barbequed, baked, or broiled. The meat contains a lot of moisture, so take extra care when deep frying since it causes the oil to pop and splatter.

SHELLFISH

The different species of shellfish, which includes crustaceans and mollusks, require specific dressing techniques. You'll need a good pair of gloves to protect your hands from the sharp edges of the shells. A Kevlar dressing glove is perfect for the chore. You'll also need a sturdy knife. The knife can be a short, flat-bladed kitchen knife, but an oyster knife is best. It features a sharp but rounded edge for ease of insertion between the shells.

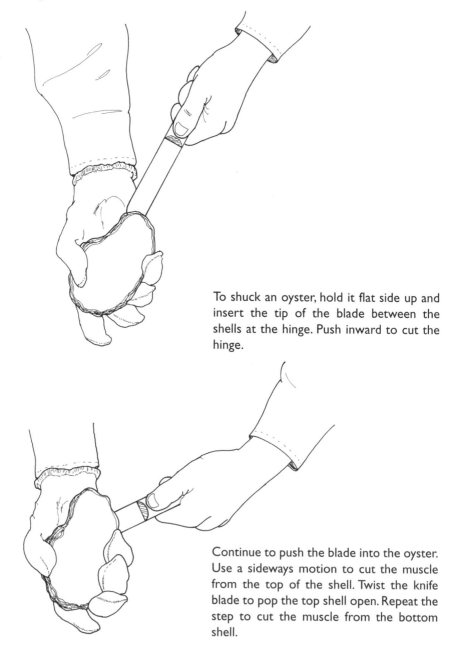

To shuck an oyster, hold it flat side up and insert the tip of the blade between the shells at the hinge. Push inward to cut the hinge.

Continue to push the blade into the oyster. Use a sideways motion to cut the muscle from the top of the shell. Twist the knife blade to pop the top shell open. Repeat the step to cut the muscle from the bottom shell.

Dressing Turtles, Frogs, Eels, Crawfish, Freshwater Shellfish, and Alligators

I n addition to freshwater and saltwater fish, other aquatic species have been traditional table fare. Some of these critters are excellent food, some are overlooked but equally good, and others are an acquired taste.

TURTLES

For most people, snapping turtles are probably one of those critters that are an acquired taste. Turtle meat, however, is excellent. The meat can be fried, baked, roasted or parboiled and made into soup or stew. Turtle afficionados suggest adding barley to the soup. Turtle meat doesn't taste like fish, but has more of the flavor and texture of frog legs.

Dressing Turtles

You'll need an old-fashioned chopping block, a hatchet and a sharp knife to dress turtles. A fairly large section of fireplace wood or tree trunk can be used as the chopping block. The first step is to kill the critter. Grasp the turtle by the tail and position it on the chopping block. In many instances the turtle will have its head withdrawn into the shell. You can sometimes trick the turtle into sticking out its head by teasing the snout with a stick. The turtle will often grab the stick and you can pull the head and neck out of the shell. With the neck extended, strike a sharp blow to the turtle's head to stun it. Then chop off the head. If you can't trick the creature into sticking out its neck, rap sharply on the top of the shell with the blunt end of a hatchet. When the head sticks out, stun him, then cut off the head. Allow it to bleed out thoroughly. Hanging by the tail can make this chore quicker. It takes time for the heart to stop beating, and the turtle to stop moving.

Two methods can be used to extract the meat from the shell. The first method is boiling and is the easiest. Fill a large kettle with water and add one tablespoon of salt per gallon of water. Bring the water to a boil. This is best done outside on a campfire, camp stove, or using a gas fish cooker or turkey fryer and a large pot. Place the turtle in the water and boil for about a half hour. Remove and use a stiff scrub brush to clean the turtle, shell, skin, and all.

Position the turtle on its back and cut off the claws, again using a hatchet. The next step is to cut the belly shell away. Locate the soft gristle areas joining the top and bottom shells together and begin cutting there. Next, cut the under-shell from the skin. Make a slit on the inside skin of each leg and skin out the legs. Skin out the

To dress snapping turtle, decapitate and boil. Cut belly shell away and skin out legs, neck, and tail.

neck and also the meat area at the base of the tail. Chop off the vent and outer part of the tail and discard. Skin out the meat at the base of the tail.

With this step the entrails are not handled, but discarded with the top shell.

Remove any fat from the meat and wash it thoroughly in cold water. Place in salt water with about one tablespoon of salt per quart of water, place in a refrigerator, and allow to cool.

You can also dress turtles without boiling, but it's a chore. You can pry away the backbone from the shell for the meat located there, but that requires a good stiff pry bar.

The meat from young turtles is fine grained and tender, but older turtles may require some tenderizing. One method is to soak overnight in a solution of ¾ water and ¼ vinegar, with a tablespoon of salt added per quart of liquid. Rinse in clean, cold water and you're ready to cook the meat.

CRAWFISH

Crawdads, crawfish, "mud puppies"—regardless of their local names these little crustaceans are delicious. Find a creek, bayou, or marsh and you'll find these tasty morsels. Make sure you check local laws regarding methods of catching. Our favorite tactic is a crawfish trap. These are available from manufacturers or you can make up your own from ½-inch mesh hardware cloth. We also seine these crustaceans from our creek, keeping the small ones for catfish trotline baits and the bigger ones for the pot. It does, however, take a pretty good number to make a meal, even the larger ones.

To cook, bring a pot of water seasoned with salt and caraway seeds to boiling, or you can add a box of purchased shrimp boil. Drop the live crawfish into the pot and when they turn red, these miniature "freshwater lobsters" are ready to eat.

Allow the crawfish to cool, then dig in. To eat, grasp the tail in one hand and the body in the other and twist and pull the tail from the body. The entrails will come out with the tail. Shuck or peel the meat from the tail. On larger crawfish you'll find the claws also have edible meat.

Some like to dip the meat in melted butter to which lemon juice has been added. A bit of garlic powder can also add to the flavor.

You can make up your own traditional "Cajun" style crawfish boil.

CAJUN CRAWFISH BOIL

½ cup of salt per gallon of water
Mustard seed
Red cayenne pepper
Bay leaves
Allspice
Cloves
Black pepper

Boil the water and above ingredients to taste with one quartered onion, garlic cloves and one cut-up lemon. Add the live crawfish to the boiling pot and cook until the crawfish turn red.

FROG LEGS

Frog legs are a popular delicacy and are served in many fine restaurants. They're also a favorite at our house. Frogging was one of my favorite pastimes as a youngster and I still enjoy the nighttime grabbing and gigging sport. The catch of a nighttime hunt can make a delicious meal. Large bull frogs are the most common quarry.

Dressing Frogs

To clean, rap the frog sharply on the head with a blunt object to kill it. Cut off the legs as close to the body as possible using a sharp, sturdy knife. The skin can be peeled off the legs quite easily with fish dressing pliers. Peel the skin down to the feet, then cut off the feet. Frog legs contain a tendon through their center. If this is not pulled out, which is quite easy to do, the legs can jump in the frying pan, surprising cooks not used to the feat. Soak the legs in cold water with a bit of vinegar for an hour or so. Rinse and cook.

Many of us like to dress the whole frog, especially the larger ones. To dress, cut through the skin behind the ears on the back of the head after killing the frog. With fish-dressing pliers, grasp this

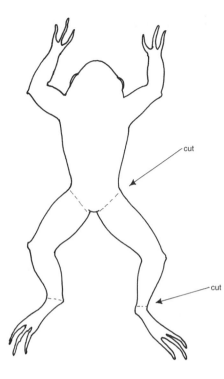

Frog legs are considered a delicacy anytime you can get them. Two methods are used: Cut off the legs at the body and cut off the feet, then skin out.

To dress a whole frog, cut through the skin behind the ears and peel the skin off with fish-dressing pliers. Cut off the front and rear feet, head, and eviscerate.

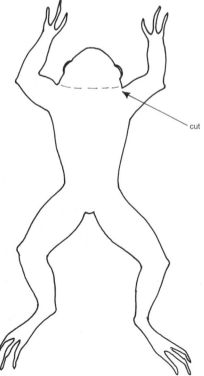

skin and pull it down and over the hind legs. Turn the frog over and peel the remaining skin back over the head and front legs. Cut off the front and rear feet as well as the head. Open the abdomen and remove the intestines. Small frogs can be cooked whole. For large frogs you may wish to cut the hind legs off, leaving the front legs and back portions together.

EELS

Considered a delicacy, eels are great tasting, but not the easiest to dress, mostly because they're so slippery and hard to hang on to. My good friend Keith Sutton catches a lot of eels on the Mississippi River and says an old time river rat gave him this method.

Kill the eel by rapping it sharply on the head, then nail its head to a board. Make a cut through the skin, behind the head, completely encircling the body. This cut should be just through the skin only, and not into the muscle. Wrap a brown paper bag or piece of bag around the eel. Squeeze the paper tightly against the eel and starting at the top, near the cut, simply pull down. The bag, skin and all will come right off.

You can also make a cut in the skin on the back from the encircling cut to the tail. Grasp the skin behind the head and peel it down to the tail with fish-dressing pliers.

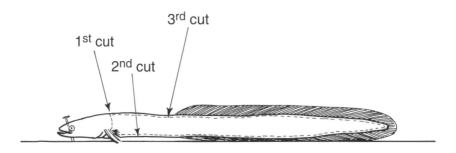

To dress an eel, stun it, and then nail the head to a board. Cut through the skin around the body behind the head and down the back. Using fish-dressing pliers, peel the skin off. Make a cut on either side of the anal and dorsal fins and peel out with the entrails. Remove head and tail.

Using a sharp fillet knife, make a fillet cut on each side of the back and anal fins and peel them out with the fish-dressing pliers. The majority of the intestines will come out with the anal fin. The fins are connected to the tail. When you reach the tail, cut off the fins and tail all in one piece.

The best method of cutting eels into cooking-sized pieces is to simply cut straight down, directly between the ribs and backbone joints. This should create pieces of a size suitable for servings and easy cooking.

The flesh of eels is delicious and can be fried, smoked, or pickled.

FRESHWATER MUSSELS

Not many folks eat freshwater mussels these days, although in times past they were a popular food, especially for the Native Americans living along rivers and streams.

It's important the mussels come only from clean, uncontaminated streams. The mussels can be boiled in the shell until they open and the meat extracted. The meat can then be used in soups and chowders, but it tends to be quite tough.

ALLIGATORS

Gator meat is excellent and can be fried, broiled, or grilled. The tail is considered the choice, but the rest of the gator is also excellent.

Dressing Alligators

Small- to medium-sized alligators are not hard to dress. Big gators take more effort. The first step is to roll the gator over on its back and make a cut from under the chin to the end of the tail. Next, cut from the first cut on the underside of the legs out to the paws. If the skin is to be marketed, make sure you dress in the manner preferred by hide buyers.

The tail meat can be filleted off or cut across the grain into steaks. The rest of the gator can be boned out and the meat cut into chunks.

Preserving Fish

Preserving fish has been a survival method from almost the beginning of mankind. Native Americans on both the West and East coasts smoked and dried salmon for winter use. They also pounded the dried meat into a powder and used it as a trade item with the Plains tribes. Egyptian hieroglyphics depict drawings of the sun, people, and various foods, detailing the methods the ancients used to preserve foods such as fish. Drying and smoking salmon is still a tradition of many Alaskan Inuits.

Fish may be preserved by several methods, including drying, smoking, pickling, canning, and freezing. The method depends on

Drying fish is one of the oldest forms of preserving. In all cases, the first step is to brine the meat.

the species, means of preserving at hand, and personal preference for how the meat will be used.

All fish to be preserved should be fresh, with no odor, and should be washed in clean water to remove any slime and blood.

DRYING FISH

Drying fish is the simplest method. As with most other foods, drying concentrates the food taste as well as the food value. The dried fish meat can then be added to soups or chowders or used in other fish recipes. Alaskan Inuits dry salmon by simply hanging it in the air, providing a staple food for themselves and their dogs. You can also dry fish in your kitchen oven or you can use a dehydrator to dry it to make fish jerky. We have used an Excaliber Dehydrator for many years, and following is their recipe for fish jerky.

FISH JERKY

Dehydrating fish is not a process to treat lightly. Fish for jerky must be extremely fresh to prevent spoilage before it can be dried. Be on the lookout for the oil content of the fish. Fatty or oily fish like tuna spoil rapidly and, unlike other meat, there is no way to simply cut off the fat. Dehydrating these types of fish is inadvisable. (See chart)

Use only fresh fish fillets that have been thoroughly cleaned, washed in fresh water, patted dry, then sliced in ¼- to ⅜-inch strips.

Curing: Make up a cold brine consisting of ¾ cup salt to 1½ quarts water and place the fish in the brine for about ½ hour. Rinse the fish thoroughly to remove all traces of salt; then arrange the pieces on a cutting board. Coat the fish with a dry cure which may be made of a combination of salt and seasonings. Layer the coated fish in an airtight glass or plastic container. Refrigerate for six to ten hours.

Remove the fish from the refrigerator and shake off any excess cure. Lay the strips on the dehydrator trays so that none are touching and dry for approximately twelve to fourteen hours at 145 degrees F.

Testing: When you squeeze the fleshy part of the cooled pieces of fish between your thumb and forefinger, it should never be crumbly or crunchy. Finish by smelling and tasting the fish. The jerky should have a mild fishy flavor and aroma. Fish jerky should contain 15 to 20 percent water and there should be no visible surface moisture. Package cooled jerky in air-tight containers such as a zip-top bag or heat-sealed vacuum bags. Store in a cool, dry place.

Fish/Shellfish	Percent Fat
*Catfish	5.2
Cod	0.5
Croaker	2.5
Flounder	1.4
Greenland Turbot	3.5
Grouper	1.0
Haddock	0.5
Halibut	4.3
*Lake trout	11.1
*Mackerel	9.9
Monkfish	1.5
*Mullet	6.0
Ocean perch	1.4
Pollock	1.3
*Rainbow trout	6.8
Rockfish	0.2
*Salmon	9.3
Sea bass	1.6
Sea trout	3.8
*Shark	5.2
Shrimp	1.6
Snapper	2.0
Sole	1.4
*Tuna	5.1
*Whitefish	7.2
Whiting	1.3
Yellow perch	1.1

*not recommended for drying

DRY CURE

1 pound salt
½ pound dark brown sugar
2 teaspoons garlic powder

2 teaspoons onion powder
1 tablespoon white ground pepper *or*
2 teaspoons ground cayenne or paprika

Thoroughly mix all ingredients, cover tightly, and allow to stand 24 hours before using. Use in the above recipe for fish jerky. Note: for a sweeter flavor, add up to one pound dark brown sugar to the above recipe. The amount of pepper can also be increased or decreased to taste.

SMOKING

Smoking is basically drying fish, but with the addition of a smoky flavor. Smoking also tends to add preservatives. The smoked fish, however, is not dried down to the low moisture content of dried fish. Smoked fish must be further preserved for long-term storage by freezing or canning.

But first, you'll need a smoker. I've tested both the Little Chief Electric Smoker from Luhr-Jensen and the Bradley Smoker. Both do

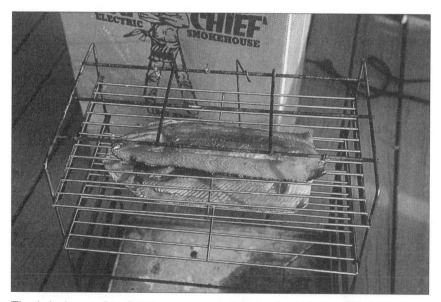

The Luhr-Jensen Big Chief smoker and their brine mixes make the chore of smoking quite easy.

an excellent job and make the chore easy and simple. You can also make your own smoker from an old refrigerator, or even a large wooden box.

As with drying, the fish should first be cured. The folks at Luhr-Jensen say almost any freshwater and saltwater fish, as well as shellfish such as clams, crayfish, mussels, scallops, shrimp, and oysters are delicious smoked with their "Easy Cure" brine solution.

If your fish must be held for some time before smoking, they should be quickly frozen. Small fish can be totally immersed in water or a light saline solution (one tablespoon salt to a quart of water) and brought to 0 degrees F. by a good cold freezer. Larger fish can be cleaned and sectioned into convenient chunks that will fit into a ½-gallon milk container and quickly frozen in the saline solution. You will also notice partially frozen fish is much easier to cut and handle.

Depending on the size and thickness of the fish you may elect to:

1. Prepare for processing by cutting fish into chunks, completely deboning as you go.
2. Fillet your fish with a thin knife, cutting above the bone layer to eliminate further deboning and then smoke the whole or proportioned fillet.
3. Simply remove the entrails and head and smoke the remaining fish whole. If you hang the whole fish in your smoker, be sure to prop open the belly cavity with a toothpick.

Always make sure your chunks, fillets, or whole fish have been neatly prepared so that they are nicely presentable when done. Cut away all unsightly material and wash the fish before brining or placing in the smoker.

Luhr-Jensen suggest two brine recipes. For their "Easy Cure" smoked fish, add ½ cup non-iodized salt and ½ cup of white sugar to one quart of water. Fill a quart jar half full with warm water. Add salt and sugar and mix well until dissolved. Then top off the jar with cold water.

Immerse the prepared fish completely in the brine solution, mixing more as needed. Brine one-inch thick chunks five to twelve hours or overnight. Brine fillets to ½-inch thick for about four hours and small whole fish or very thin fillets about two to four hours.

Stir the solution and rotate fish occasionally. Remove from the brine. Rinse each piece in cool water and place on paper towels. Pat dry.

In about an hour you will notice a tacky glaze on the surface of the fish. This is called the "pellicle." Your fish is now ready for loading into the Little Chief Smoker.

Load the smoker with the fish. Plug in the smoker and smoke thick chunks for eight to twelve hours, using three pans of Chips 'n Chunks flavor fuel. For fillets to ½-inch thick, smoke five to eight hours using two pans of wood chips. For small fish or thin pieces, smoke two to four hours, using one to two pans of wood chips.

Add Chips 'n Chunks wood chips to the smoke pan during the early stages of the drying cycle. Check the meat periodically for the degree of doneness desired.

For oily fish with a stronger flavor use the Little Chief Smoked Fish brine. These fish include cod, bass, pike, tuna types, barracuda, mackerel, eels, squid, and octopus. Soak in brine for at least four hours, rinse and dry.

LITTLE CHIEF SMOKED FISH BRINE

2 quarts water
1 cup non-iodized salt
½ cup brown sugar
2 tablespoons lemon concentrate *or*
¼ cup lemon juice
¼ tablespoon garlic powder
¼ tablespoon onion powder

Smoke four to ten hours using three to five pans of hickory, apple, or alder chips.

Little Chief Smoked Salmon Deluxe recipe is recommended for Chinook and Coho salmon as well as steelhead and other large trout.

LITTLE CHIEF SMOKED SALMON DELUXE

Soak fish chunks for eight or more hours in the refrigerator in a brine consisting of:

⅓ cup sugar
¼ cup non-iodized salt
2 cups soy sauce

1 cup water
½ teaspoon onion powder
½ teaspoon garlic powder
½ teaspoon pepper
½ teaspoon tabasco sauce
1 cup dry white wine

Use two to three pans of hickory, alder, or a mixture of apple and cherry and leave in the smoker until drying is completed. This may take twelve hours, depending on the thickness of the meat.

Place largest and thickest chunks on the bottom rack.

Fish smoked in this manner will keep in your refrigerator for up to two weeks. For further storage, the smoked fish should be wrapped and frozen.

BRADLEY'S FAMOUS HOT SMOKED SALMON

The Bradley Smoker has a thermometer and the heat can be regulated by moving a switch. The Bradley Smoker also has a unique smoking method utilizing discs of compressed wood chips that are continually fed into the smoker. It's an extremely easy smoker to use. Following is their recipe for salmon:

Dry rub ingredients:
Cure (white sugar and salt)
Vegetable oil
Garlic and Onion (salt or powder), or dill, ginger, or dry mustard
Coarse pepper
Dried parsley or chive flakes

Leave skin on the salmon fillets. If the fillets are over one-inch thick, perforate skin every two to three inches with point of a sharp knife. If the fillets are over 1½ inches thick, in addition to perforating the skin, also slash the flesh ¼ to ⅜ inch deep, parallel and running in the direction of the rib lines. Rub or brush the fillets with a liberal amount of vegetable oil. Sprinkle cure heavily and evenly on the oiled flesh. Use enough cure so that it doesn't become soaked through with oil. Sprinkle garlic and onion (salt or powder) over the flesh. Rub the spices and cure lightly into it, including the cut surfaces, to even out the spices. Sprinkle coarse pepper on the flesh. Wrap two similar sized salmon fillets, flesh to flesh, and store in

The Bradley Smoker features an infinite heat control and utilizes flavored bisquettes.

plastic bag or plastic container that is tightly covered. Leave salmon sides in cure and refrigerate for fourteen to twenty hours.

To smoke, place the cured salmon, skin side down, on oiled racks in the Bradley Smoker. Rub the flesh to even the residual cure. Sprinkle parsley flakes or chives over the flesh if desired and place the racks in the smoker. First start the Smoke Generator at a very low temperature, 100 to 120 degrees F., for one to two hours. Then increase the temperature to 140 degrees F. for two to four hours and finish at 175 degrees F. for one to two hours. The fish is cooked when the temperature of the flesh is a minimum of 140 degrees F. Bradley's Famous Hot Smoked Salmon will refrigerate for two to three weeks when securely wrapped in aluminum foil.

Serve Bradley's Famous Hot Smoked Salmon with baguettes, capers and onions, or crackers and cream cheese. You can also mix it in with your favorite pasta, or make into mousse or pate.

Storage of Smoked Fish

According to the booklet, *Proper Processing of Wild Game and Fish*, by Penn State College of Agricultural Sciences, Agricultural Research and Cooperative Extension,

> Fish smoked without proper salting and cooking, though, can cause food poisoning. The bacteria that cause botulism food poisoning could start to grow after two to three weeks in refrigeration. For long-term storage, smoked fish must be frozen or canned. Canning is preferred by many who smoke fish at home, and the fish must be processed in a pressure canner to destroy *Colstridium botulinum* spores. Unfortunately, the length of processing time needed to guarantee safety can affect the quality of home-canned smoked fish. Canning tends to dry the flesh, darken the color and intensify the smoked flavor; reducing the processing time to lessen these undesirable quality changes is unsafe. Instead, the smoking procedure must be modified.
>
> For best quality, fish that will be canned should be smoked for a shorter time than ready-to-eat products. Lightly smoked fish must be promptly canned to assure that it will be safe and top quality. It should not be eaten before it is canned, as some bacteria survive the short smoking process and are destroyed only

during canning. If you plan to can your fish, the following smoking procedure will give the best results.

Different species of fish require different preparation techniques. Salmon usually are prepared by removing the backbone and splitting them. Bones usually are not removed. Rockfish and flatfish such as sole, cod, and flounder should be filleted.

You'll need about ⅔ pounds of smoked fish for each one-pint canning jar. About 1½ to 3 pounds of whole fish will yield this amount of smoked fish, depending on the amount of waste removed such as the head, tail, fins and entrails. Be sure to use good quality, firm fish. Smoking and canning won't improve poor quality! Keep fish refrigerated or on ice before smoking.

FISH SAUSAGE

Fish meat can also be ground and made into "sausage." This is a good method of utilizing "rough" fish, such as carp, buffalo, suckers or redhorse. The fish should be skinned and deboned, or fillets cut from the fish. Fish that have Y bones should be scored about ¼ inch apart. The fillets will grind best if partially frozen. Grind through a fine or ³⁄₁₆-inch plate. Several methods can be used after the meat has been ground.

- Method One: Mix ¼ pound of ground beef and one teaspoon salt and ¼ teaspoon each garlic powder, onion powder, and black pepper for each pound of ground fish. Sage or red peppers are also common sausage spices and may be added to taste. Mix all ingredients well and form into patties. The patties should be placed in a refrigerator for 24 hours to allow the sausage to "bind." The patties can then be frozen or cooked immediately. To cook, fry in a skillet over medium heat about four to five minutes per side. Make sure you do not overcook.
- Method Two: Bacon is added instead of ground beef. For each five pounds of fish add 1½ pounds of bacon and 12 soda crackers. Grind the bacon and fish in a fine grinder, then run the crackers through the grinder. Not only does this clean out the grinder, but pulverizes the crackers. Add ½ cup powdered milk, ½ cup water and 5 teaspoons salt, 1 teaspoon each garlic powder, onion powder, and black pepper. Cayenne pepper or

tabasco sauce may also be added to taste. Mix all ingredients together and shape into rolls. Place on a piece of waxed paper on a flat pan and place in the freezer. The roll can be sliced while frozen and then fried.

CANNING FISH

Fresh fish can also be preserved by pressure canning. We've canned carp, buffalo, and other rough fish for many years. This softens the tiny, impossible to remove bones in these fish, making the bones edible. The meat is then used in fish patties, fish loaf, or in casseroles. It's another great way of utilizing these rough fish. Canning also offers several advantages. The heat from canning inactivates the enzymes that degrade muscle tissue. Precooked, canned foods are ready to eat. Canning also avoids the problems of freezer burn and fish flesh drying out in the freezer.

Fish must be canned in a pressure canner if the meat is to be safe to eat. Use only pint or half-pint, not quart jars. If the meat has been frozen, thaw the fish in a refrigerator, then process immediately. Cut the fish into chunks. The bones can be left in if desired—they add nutrition and flavor. Fill the jars, leaving one inch of headspace. If the skins are left on, place with the skins to the outside of the jar. Add ½ to 1 teaspoon salt per pint or ¼ to ½ teaspoon salt per half-pint jar. Do not, however, add liquid. Adjusts lids and process according to your canning booklet or check with your local extension office for current information. Your local extension office will also check your pressure canner gauge for accuracy.

The National Food Safety Database web site states that glass-like crystals of magnesium ammonium phosphate sometimes form in canned salmon. There is no way for the home canner to prevent these crystals from forming, but they usually dissolve when heated and are safe to eat.

The Web site, www.homecanning.com, sponsored by Ball and Kerr brand canning equipment, suggests that instead of adding salt to the jars of salmon or shad, pre-soak the fish in a brine. Dissolve one cup salt in one gallon water to make a brine. Let the cut-up fish chunks soak in the brine for one hour. Pack as above with no added liquid (or salt) and process half-pint and pint jars according to current recommendations.

"Mock" Salmon

The South Dakota State University Extension offers the following recipes for "Mock" Salmon and Quick Pink Salmon which are excellent uses for many of the rough fish species.

"MOCK" SALMON

Allow 2¼ to 3 pounds of whole fish for each pint of canned fish. Clean and prepare fish. Remove heads, fins, and tails. Remove skin, if desired. If the fish is slimy, a solution of 1 tablespoon vinegar to 2 quarts water helps remove the slime. The color of some fish can be improved by soaking the fish in water containing ½ cup salt to 1 gallon water for 30 minutes. Do not reuse salt water. Rinse fish in clean water. Cut fish into jar-sized lengths. Make a sauce.

Sauce:
1 cup catsup
1 cup vinegar
½ cup water
3 tablespoons salt
¼ cup minced onion
2 bay leaves, crumbled

Combine and heat the above ingredients. This makes enough sauce for about 8 pints. Pack fish into jars to within 1 inch of the top. Cover with sauce, leaving 1 inch headspace. Remove air bubbles, wipe jar rims, place prepared lids on jars and tighten the screw bands. Proceed according to canning time table.

QUICK PINK SALMON

To each pint of fish add:

1 tablespoon vinegar
¼ teaspoon salt
2 tablespoons tomato juice

Leave 1 inch headspace. Adjust lids. Process according to the table for fish.

Pickling Fish

Fish are also often pickled. This, however, should not be confused with curing fish in brine and then drying. Pickling involves the use of vinegar and although only a few species are commercially pickled, almost any fish species can be preserved at home using this method. The pickled fish must be stored in a refrigerator at 40 to 45 degrees F. and must be used within four to five weeks.

The South Dakota State University Extension Service recommends that when pickling, use only drinking water or water approved under all sanitary codes. "Hard" waters are unsuitable, especially those with a high iron, calcium, or magnesium content. The minerals can interfere with the curing process and cause rancidity and off flavors. Use only a high-grade, white distilled vinegar of five percent acidity (50 grain). Acidity is listed on the label. Do not use vinegars of unknown acidity. Ciders and other fruit vinegars may give the fish an off flavor and color. A high-grade, pure granulated dairy or canning non-iodized salt should also be used. The salt must be as free as possible from magnesium compounds, because these give a bitter flavor to the cured product, and also cause discoloration of the fish. Table sugar such as cane or beet is recommended and the spices should be fresh and of a high grade of purity. Prepared, commercial mixtures are convenient and time-saving if you can obtain the amount desired. The procedure is quite simple. Soak fresh fish in a weak brine of one cup of salt to a gallon of cold water for one hour.

Then drain and pack fish in a glass, heavy food-grade plastic or enamel container. Add a strong brine of 2½ pounds salt to 1 gallon of water for 12 hours. Keep refrigerated.

PICKLED FISH

10 pounds fish
1 ounce whole allspice
1 ounce mustard seed
2 ounces regular mixed pickling spice
½ pound onion, sliced
½ ounce bay leaves
1½ quarts distilled white vinegar

2½ pints water
1 ounce white pepper
1 ounce hot ground or dried peppers (optional)

Rinse the fish in fresh water. Combine the ingredients listed above in a large pan or kettle. Bring to a boil and add fish. Simmer for 10 minutes, or until flesh is easily pierced with a fork. Remove fish from the liquid and place in a single layer on a flat pan and refrigerate for rapid cooling to prevent spoilage. Pack cold in a clean glass jar, adding a few spices, a bay leaf, freshly sliced onions, and, if desired, a slice of lemon. Strain the vinegar, bring to a boil, and pour into jars until the fish is covered. Adjust lids. This product must be stored in the refrigerator at 40 to 45 degrees F. and should be used within four to six weeks.

"Carp In North America" published by the American Fisheries Society in 1987 recommends pickling as an excellent use of this prolific rough fish.

PICKLED CARP

Small pieces of carp make excellent pickles (one of the oldest forms of food preservation known). In some regions, pickled carp has replaced pickled herring as an appetizer at dinner clubs and restaurants. Jars of pickled fish can be refrigerated where they will be good for weeks. They make unique gifts too, and can be dressed with sliced, stuffed olives and brightly colored strips of pimento and sweet pickles. Carp prepared this way make a tart-sweet, chewy delicacy.

For each quart of fresh carp chunks, dissolve ⅝ cup of pickling salt in enough vinegar to cover the fish. Let stand four to six days at about 40 degrees F. Drain off salt solution and rinse thoroughly with cold water. Then collect

1 pint white vinegar
1 pint white port wine
¾ cup sugar
⅛ oz. pickling spice
Sliced onions

Place alternate layers of fish and onions in sterilized jars. Place hot mixture of vinegar, wine, sugar, and pickling spice over fish. Refrigerate and let stand one week before using. This solution covers

4 quarts of fish. For variety, drain the juices after the process is complete and replace with commercial sour cream. A real treat.

FREEZING FISH

One of the most common methods of preserving fish these days is freezing. Freezing is fast and easy, but there are some disadvantages and special steps must be taken to assure quality meat. Fish flesh tends to dry out more quickly than other meats and this causes it to freezer burn quicker. Wrap the fish carefully to maintain quality as long as possible. Heavy-duty freezer paper or aluminum foil are equally effective, though foil is easier to mold around odd-shaped pieces. Plastic zippered freezer bags are also convenient options. One tactic is to first wrap in plastic wrap, then double wrap in freezer paper or aluminum foil.

When wrapping fish, squeeze as much air from the packages as possible. When small pieces are to be frozen together, as with fish fillets, air is best eliminated by using water packs. To freeze in water, fill a container, such as a milk carton, with water. Add whole fish, filets or chunks and cover the fish with water, then seal and freeze. Whole dressed fish freezes best in this manner.

Fish can also be glazed with ice for longer storage. Place the cleaned, eviscerated fish on a tray and place in the freezer. Once the fish are frozen dip in near freezing water to glaze coat them. Then place back in the freezer to allow the glaze to freeze. Repeat the dipping process until the fish is covered with about ⅛ inch of ice. Then double wrap in plastic wrap and freezer paper or aluminum foil.

Fish can also be gelatin coated to prevent freezer burn. Add ¼ cup of lemon juice to a pint of water, then pour off one half cup of the mixture and dissolve a packet of unflavored gelatin in it. Bring the remaining liquid to a boil and stir in the dissolved gelatin. Allow to cool to room temperature, then dip the fish meat in the mixture. Allow to drain for a few seconds, then wrap in heavy-duty protective plastic wrap. Double wrap with freezer paper and label and date, then place in the quick-freeze compartment of your freezer.

Following is a general rule for storage times with proper preparation for storage.

- Large lean fish, whole: 6 months
- Large lean fish, fillets: 4 months
- Small lean fish, whole: 4 months
- Small lean fish, fillets: 3 months
- Shellfish: 3 months

It is extremely important to properly prepare and freeze shellfish. The quicker you can freeze shellfish after their harvest, the longer they will store in the freezer. Shuck scallops and freeze in air-tight containers. Oysters and clams can also be shucked and frozen in the same manner. The best method, however, with oysters and clams is to leave them in their shells. They're easier to shuck when thawed and there is no loss of juices. Clean and cook blue crabs before freezing. The best method is to freeze the claws and cores, then thaw and remove the meat. Shrimp should be headed, and frozen in containers of water.

Vacuum Packing

One of the easiest methods of extending freezer storage time is to use a vacuum packing system such as the FoodSaver Professional II model from Tilia. Research conducted by an independent microbiological research company showed that vacuum packaging in Food-Saver Bags provides far greater protection against freezer burn than the leading brand of reclosable plastic food storage bags. After four weeks of the study, the meat in FoodSaver Bags showed no weight loss, ice crystal formation, or visible freezer burn.

The reason fish loses its fresh-tasting quality, even in the freezer, is the presence of oxygen, which causes freezer burn. Another study by the University of California Department of Food Science and Technology showed that fish have a shelf life of two years in a freezer when vacuum packaged, compared with six months with no vacuum packing.

We've tested the FoodSaver Professional II, Tilia's largest model, which uses a powerful piston pump to create a vacuum of commercial quality. We've used the unit for everything from shrimp to crappie and mahi-mahi fillets. You do have to be careful not to puncture the bags if bones are left in the fish.

The patented FoodSaver 3-ply, FDA-approved bags and rolls are made of plastic with a nylon outer layer. They are strong and won't leak, so the vacuum stays intact and the food stays fresh for months or even years in the freezer. The bags can be boiled, microwaved, cleaned (even in a dishwasher), and reused. Bags can also be custom-made to fit the length of your catch.

The FoodSaver is ideal for packaging fish and seafood because it has a special feature that makes a tight seal even when there is excess liquid. Plus, you can vacuum package more than 50 bags at a time without any problem, especially important when freezing many fillets, steaks or whole fish. The fish, however, still need to be frozen, even when vacuum packed.

When fish is prepared in meal-size portions, it's put inside a bag, a vacuum is pulled, and the bag is sealed, with all the air, odors, and foreign tastes left outside. The compact, finished package can be easily weighed and marked with the date, description, and weight, all with no mess.

Cooking Fish

Fish is a very versatile meat. It can be baked, broiled, grilled, stewed, poached, sauteed, pan fried, deep fried, smoked, pickled, canned, or even cooked in a microwave. The cooking choice depends on the cooking methods available, the species of fish, and personal preferences. Although most fish can be cooked by any of the standard means mentioned, some varieties are best cooked in specific methods. The fat content of fish varies a great deal. Those with low fat content, such as crappie, are best poached or deep-fried to keep moisture in or to add moisture. Fish with a moderate fat content can be cooked in almost any manner. Fish with a high fat content are best grilled or broiled. Fish with a higher fat content can also be baked, but they should not be basted during the cooking process. It's fairly easy to determine the general fat content of any fish. Fish with a mild flavor and white or extremely light meat are lower in fat. The darker and the more solid the meat, the higher the fat content. Tuna, for instance, has a very high fat content.

All fish flesh, however, is more delicate than most other meats. Fish cooks very quickly and can easily be overcooked. When properly done, the flesh of fish flakes easily. To test for doneness, push the tines of a fork into the flesh at about a 45-degree angle and lift up to see if it flakes. It should also be opaque. If the flesh is still translucent and doesn't lift up or flake easily, it's not done. Overcooked fish on the other hand, also won't flake properly and is usually tough and extremely dry. The different species of fish also cook differently. For instance, crappie flakes more easily than tuna. The U.S. FDA recommends cooking fish until it reaches an internal temperature of 145 degrees F. If you are having trouble determining doneness by flaking, double check a few times with a thermometer.

Shore-side lunch is the best method of cooking fish. The fish are the absolute freshest and the outdoor experience only adds to the great taste.

With a little experience cooking your favorite species, you'll learn the test for the best flaking and doneness.

The best fish and shellfish, of course, is fresh. If you haven't enjoyed a shore lunch of freshly caught fish, then you haven't tasted fish at its finest. Fish and shellfish, however, are quite often frozen until you're ready to cook. Do not thaw frozen fish at room temperature. Fish and shellfish both spoil and become unsafe to eat very quickly. Thaw fish or shellfish in their unopened packages in a refrigerator for six to eight hours. In some cases this may require overnight thawing. If you must defrost fish quickly, immerse the unopened package in cold water for about an hour or microwave on the "defrost" setting, stopping when the fish still has ice crystals. Never leave raw or cooked fish or shellfish at room temperature longer than an hour. Hold hot foods above 140 degrees F. and cold foods below 40 degrees F.

Cleanliness and safety is just as important when preparing fish as in preparing red meats. Always marinate fish in the refrigerator. Always discard marinade after use because it contains uncooked fish juices that may contain bacteria. Do not let raw fish or juices touch cooked, ready-to-serve foods. Wash all utensils and cutting surfaces that have been used to prepare raw fish with hot, soapy water before using for ready-to-serve foods.

Following are general cooking tips for the various methods of cooking fish. The following chapter provides a variety of specific fish and seafood recipes.

PAN FRYING OR SAUTEEING

Pan frying is very simple and a tradition for shore lunch. Some of the best trout and walleye I've tasted have been fried on shore shortly after they were caught. It's important to have the proper skillet for frying fish. The fish can be fried in deep fat, or with just enough cooking oil to cover the bottom of the skillet. The latter is usually the most popular choice. Although aluminum skillets can be used, the best skillet for pan-frying fish is a cast iron skillet. These are heavy and tend to provide more even heat. If you're backpacking or canoeing, however, a lighter weight skillet may be preferred.

Fish can be pan fried in oil, with olive oil the most healthful choice. Regardless of the cooking oil used, it must be very hot, but

Pan frying is a great way of cooking fish, whether in camp or at home.

not smoking. If the oil is not hot enough the fish will come out tough and greasy. If the oil is too hot, the fish will have a burned taste. To test the cooking oil for the correct temperature, drop a bread crumb into the hot oil. If the bread crumb bubbles and floats around, you can place the fish into the oil. Do not add all the fish pieces at once because this causes the oil to cool too quickly. Add just one piece at a time, making sure the fish pieces continue bubbling vigorously in the oil. Once they turn golden brown on one side, turn them over and cook the opposite side. Once both sides are golden brown, the fish is done. You can also test for flakiness with a fork.

Remove the fish from the skillet and place on paper towels to drain. The paper towels will absorb any excess fat.

Fish for pan frying can be dipped or rolled in a variety of batters, or the pieces can be fried without a coating. Whether you coat the fish pieces or not, you'll probably wish to add some salt, pepper, and spices to the fish before cooking.

Sprinkling a little lemon juice over the fish pieces adds to the taste. One of our favorite methods is to lightly salt, then sprinkle lemon-pepper over the pieces before frying. If adding a dry coating of flour, corn meal, crumbs, or a combination, the easiest method of applying the coating is to place the coating mixture in a plastic bag along with the salt, pepper, and spices desired. Then place the fish, a few pieces at a time, in the bag, close the top and shake well. This evenly coats the fish pieces with no mess.

Sautéing is lightly frying over a low flame in butter or margarine. This may be done with skinned or scaled fish or even with fish with the skin left on as in the case of small trout. Properly done, the flesh will be lightly browned on both sides. Skin-on sautéed fish will have a slightly browned but not burned skin.

Deep Frying

Except for shore lunches and while camping, I prefer deep frying rather than pan-frying most fish. Properly done, deep-frying holds in the moisture, and results in a less "greasy" meat since the flash frying prevents the meat from absorbing the cooking oil. Deep-frying is also a popular method when you need to feed a crowd. In fact, two deep fryers serve over a hundred pounds of catfish during our annual church fish fries.

You can deep fry in a large pan on a stove, and our family did that for many years. The pan should be a heavy duty model to allow for even heating of the oil and to prevent burning. The best method involves a deep fryer, designed just for the purpose. Several electric models are available with built-in temperature gauges, which are extremely important. My personal choice, however, is an outside, gas fish fryer. I have a Bass Pro fish cooker with a stainless steel fry pan and basket that I've been using for many years. These types of cookers are also available with aluminum cooking pans and baskets. Some prefer cookers with cast iron dutch ovens instead of the aluminum or stainless steel because the cast iron disperses the heat more efficiently. I've also cooked with the cast iron models and they do make it easier to maintain a steady temperature over a long cooking period. All the outside models are fueled by propane bottles and are available with different size cooking pans ranging from 8 to 10½ quarts. Most cookers also come with a lift-out basket that sits down in the cooker. When the fish is done, merely lift out the basket by the handle and dump the fish out onto paper toweling to absorb any excess oil. A deep-fry thermometer that attaches to the side of the fry pot is a necessity for consistently successful fish frying. A good, clean oil is also extremely important. Vegetable oil can be used, but many prefer to use peanut oil instead because it doesn't smoke as quickly at higher temperatures. It doesn't have an off flavor as do some oils and it also contains no cholesterol. The oil should be clean without burned particles from previous frying sessions.

Oil for deep-frying fish must be very hot, almost to the smoking point. The correct temperature for fish frying is 375 degrees F. and in most instances you will have to adjust the fryer flame to maintain the proper temperature. Gas fish fryers can provide a lot of heat and it's important to bring the temperature up gradually to prevent burning the oil. If you don't have a deep-fry thermometer, a one inch cube of bread can be used to determine if the temperature is high enough. If the oil turns the bread chunk golden brown in a minute, the oil is sufficiently hot. It's a good idea to cook only a few pieces of fish at a time, even when cooking for a crowd. Filling the pot with fish not only decreases the temperature, but also adds the risk of the hot oil boiling over out of the pot. If using frozen fish, make sure the pieces are thoroughly thawed so you don't have water added to the grease, which causes the grease to pop and

One of the most popular methods of cooking is deep frying with fish fryers. It's easy and you can easily feed a crowd.

Any number of commercial fish fry mixes are available, or you can mix your own.

foam. Pat the fish dry before battering or coating to remove as much water as possible. Some fish naturally contains a lot of water and they tend to pop when fried.

Fish for deep frying are usually dipped or rolled in a fish or tempura batter. The following chapter has a number of recipes for some basic fish dips.

Caution: Cooking with smoking hot oil should not be taken lightly. You can be killed or very badly burned with hot oil. Take all precautions, whether you're pan frying, deep frying in the house on a stove, using an electric deep fry, or an outside gas deep fryer. Do not allow the oil to boil over onto the open flame. If cooking oil catches on fire do not use water to extinguish the fire. Use a fire extinguisher or baking soda or a pan lid to suffocate a fire inside a pot.

GRILLING

Cooking over hot coals is also a very popular and productive method of cooking many types of fish and shellfish. Those with solid meat, such as tuna or shark, grill the best. Light, flaky fish such as crappie or bass fillets can also be grilled if the pieces are held in a fish grilling basket. These baskets clamp down on both sides of the fish and allow you to easily turn the fish. If using a grilling basket, coat both sides with vegetable oil, or spray-on coating before using to prevent the fish from sticking to the basket. Small fish such as crappie, bass, flounder, weakfish, mackerel, snappers or small bluefish can be grilled whole. Merely coat with vegetable oil and season with salt and pepper. You can also add Tabasco sauce for more flavor. Place in a grilling basket, alternating heads and tails to preserve space, and cook over a medium heat with the fish about three inches from the coals. Grill for four to six minutes, turn and grill another four to six minutes or until done. Baste with melted butter or margarine during the last few minutes of grilling on each side. Herb-flavored butters can add interesting flavors.

Fish species such as salmon, pollock, haddock, halibut, bluefish, tuna, and shark are often cut into steaks and grilled. You won't need the basket when grilling steaks. You will, however, need to oil the steaks as well as the grill. Cut one-inch thick steaks and place on the grill about three inches from the charcoal of a medium fire. Grill six minutes, turn and grill another six minutes, or until done. Salt and pepper to taste or sprinkle with lemon pepper. For additional flavor, marinate the steaks in Italian salad dressing for about an hour before grilling. Fish should be grilled in an uncovered grill. Both whole fish and fish steaks should be sear-cooked one to two minutes per side over direct heat, then moved to indirect heat to finish grilling. Again, basting with butter or oil will keep the fish moist.

BAKING

Health conscious folks often prefer baked fish and some baked-fish dishes are a tradition. Almost any fish species can be baked. Fatty species such as striped bass, king mackerel, salmon, large mullet, and bluefish are good for baking. Small pieces, fillets, steaks, and chunks can be baked, but whole fish often provides the best baked fish. Whole baked fish may also be stuffed. To bake small pieces, fillets, and steaks, lay the pieces in a single layer in a greased, shallow baking dish or pan. Brush melted butter or margarine over the pieces and season to taste. Do not cover the pan. Bake in a preheated 450°F. oven until fish flakes done. This could take as little as under five minutes for thin fillets to approximately ten minutes for a one-inch thick steak.

For larger, whole fish, coat the inside and outside with melted butter or margarine and add seasonings of your choice. Bake in 450°F. oven until done.

Specific recipes for baking fish with coatings, stuffings and different seasonings, follow in the next chapter.

POACHING FISH

Poaching is cooking in liquid. Many delicate-flavored fish species can be poached to produce gourmet fare. Firm-fleshed, larger fish, such as halibut, cod, and salmon are often poached in court-bouillon. For the most part, poaching is an easy cooking method, requiring few specialty cooking tools. You can use either a special fish poaching pan or a roaster or skillet. Several different liquids or combinations of liquids along with spices and other ingredients can be used for poaching. Place enough liquid in the pan to cover half of the fish. Bring the liquid to a boil. Carefully lower the fish on a greased rack into the liquid. Return the liquid to a boil, then turn down the heat and simmer until the fish is done.

STEAMED FISH

Steaming is also done with liquid, except the fish is kept up and out of the liquid and cooked only by its steam. Steaming can be done by making a rack or a trivet with legs. The rack must be placed in a large roaster with about a quart of water. The rack must not, however, be submerged in the water. Place the rack in the roaster and bring the water to a boil. Place the fish on the rack, salt and pepper to taste, and add seasonings. Place a cover on the roaster and keep the liquid boiling. Steam for ten to twelve minutes or until the fish flakes easily.

BROILING FISH

Turn on the broiler and bring it to a high heat. Place the fish on a broiler rack or grid or in a well-greased, oven-proof cooking dish. Broil three to four inches from the heat source until the fish is browned on top and done. This will usually take about five minutes per ½ inch of fish thickness. Test with a fork, and if the fish is not quite done, turn off the broiler and close the door to allow the fish to cook for a few more minutes. You may have to turn large (over ½ inch thick) fish over halfway through the broiling process. Most whole fish will require turning to evenly broil both sides. Basting with a butter- or oil-based sauce will keep broiled fish moist.

MICROWAVE

Small fish fillets and equal-sized pieces of larger fish fillets are easily cooked in the microwave. Cook in a shallow, microwave-safe dish covered with plastic wrap that is vented in one corner. Allow approximately three minutes per pound of fillets and rotate dish or cook on a turntable.

CAMPFIRE FISH

Broiled

Fish can also be cooked by a campfire, even without the modern conveniences. Fish with solid meat, such as salmon or lake trout are best, but walleye and even bass or catfish will work. Two broiling methods can be used. Skewering the fish is the simplest, and a time-honored method. Larger fish should be butterfly filleted. Be sure to leave the skin on; it helps hold the cooked fish together. Small trout and others can be skewered whole. Green hardwood sticks about the size of your finger are used to hold the fish. Sharpen both ends of the sticks and peel off the bark. Skewer the fish. Additional small sticks about ¼-inch thick can be used to spread out fillets if necessary. Lean the skewered fish against a horizontal bar or other item, or simply stick in the ground close to or over the fire. Baste with butter and salt and pepper to taste. Skewered fish will normally take about a half hour to cook, depending on the heat from the coals and the distance the fish are positioned from the fire.

Larger fish are best cooked on a plank. Cut a half log or better yet, split a plank from a sweet hardwood such as oak. Butterfly the fish by cutting through the back, removing the insides, but leaving the skin intact. Brace the plank up against the coals of a campfire and allow it to heat up. When the plank has warmed, move it away from the fire and fasten the fish skin-side down on the plank with nails or slivers of green wood driven into holes cut with a sharp

Small fish can be skewered and cooked over the campfire.

Larger fish should be fastened to a plank and reflector cooked.

knife in the plank. Prop the plank and fish up close to the fire. Creating a reflector fire with back logs will speed up the cooking process. Cook until the fish flakes easily. Baste with butter and add salt and pepper to taste.

Steamed Fish

Fish, especially small whole fish such as panfish or trout, can be steamed in camp. Clean, eviscerate, or fillet. Wrap each individual piece of fish in parchment paper. Wrap the parchment wrapped pieces into one bundle using several sheets of newspaper. Place the entire bundle of newspaper wrapped fish in water until the newspaper is thoroughly soaked. Scrape a layer of hot coals back from the fire, place the fish bundle on the scraped area and cover with hot coals. Allow the fish to steam in the newspaper for 15 to 20 minutes. The newspaper will char, but the parchment paper will remain intact.

FISH SPECIES

One of the most important aspects in successfully cooking fish is choosing the correct cooking method for each species. Following are the most popular fish and shellfish, and the best methods of preparing and cooking them.

Freshwater Fish

BASS: LARGEMOUTH, SPOTTED, AND SMALLMOUTH

Fillet or skin and draw. Fat content is low, flesh medium soft, flavor is mild. Bass can be fried, baked, and broiled. Bass can also be grilled, but a fish basket must be used because the flesh falls apart easily.

BLUEGILL AND SUNFISH

Fillet, skin and draw, or scale and draw. Fat content is low, flesh soft, flavor delicate. Best method of cooking is pan- or deep-frying.

CRAPPIE

Fillet. Fat content is low, flesh soft, flavor delicate. Best cooking method is pan or deep frying.

TROUT

Draw—leave skin on, cook whole. Fat content ranges from moderate to high, depending on species. Flesh is firm but has a delicate flavor. Bake, broil, grill, smoke, or pan fry for a shore lunch.

WALLEYE AND SAUGER

Fillet or skin and draw. Fat content is low, flesh has a firm texture, flavor is delicate. Walleye and sauger can be cooked in almost any manner, except grilling—unless a basket is used.

WHITE BASS/HYBRID

Fillet and remove red meat. Fat content is moderate to high, flesh is firm, flavor moderate to strong. Deep frying is best cooking method.

STRIPED BASS

Fillet, steak, chunk, or skin and draw and leave whole. Remove red meat. Fat content is moderate to high, flesh firm, flavor moderate to strong. Can be fried or baked.

CATFISH: CHANNEL, BLUE, WHITE, FLATHEAD

Fillet, skin, chunk, steak, or skin and draw. Fat content, low to moderate, texture is firm, flavor is mild. Can be baked, broiled, smoked, pan fried, or deep fried. Deep frying is most popular.

FRESHWATER DRUM

Fillet or skin and draw. Fat content is low, flesh firm, flavor mild. Deep fry or bake.

CARP AND BUFFALO

Skin and draw, chunk, or cook whole. Fat content is moderate, flesh is firm, flavor mild to strong. Deep fry, bake, broil, smoke, pickle, or can.

SUCKERS

Skin or scale and draw, fillet, or chunk. Fat content is low, flesh firm, flavor is delicate. Scoring to cut tiny bones and deep frying is the most popular method. Can be pickled, smoked, or canned.

MUSKELLUNGE, NORTHERN PIKE, PICKEREL

Fillet, steak, chunk, or skin and draw. Low fat content, flesh firm, flavor mild. Pan fry, deep fry, bake, broil or smoke.

PADDLEFISH

Skin and draw, fillet, steak, or chunk. Remove red blood line meat. Fat content low, flesh firm, flavor mild. Can be grilled, smoked, baked, broiled, or fried. Roe is a prized delicacy.

BOWFIN

Skin and draw, chunk, or fillet. Fat content low, flesh soft, flavor strong. Deep fry or smoke.

GAR

Skin, fillet then cut fillets into chunks. Fat content low, flesh firm, flavor mild. Stew, grind into fish cakes, deep fry, stir fry, or bake.

STURGEON

Skin, draw, fillet, chunk, or steak. Fat content low, flesh firm, flavor mild. Deep fry, bake, broil, or smoke. Roe is a prized delicacy.

AMERICAN EEL

Skin and draw, or chunk. Fat content low, flesh firm, flavor mild. Poach, stew, bake, fry, pickle, or smoke.

LAKE PERCH

Skin or scale and draw, fillet, chunk. Fat content low, flesh firm, flavor mild. Deep fry or pan fry, saute, bake or broil.

AMERICAN SMELT

Draw or leave whole. Fat content high, flesh firm, flavor mild to strong. Pan fry or deep fry, broil whole, or smoke.

WHITEFISH

Skin and draw, fillet, steak, or chunk. Fat content high, flesh firm, flavor delicate. Fry, bake, broil, or stew.

Other

TURTLES

Skin and dress. Fat content low, flesh firm, flavor mild to moderate. Stew, broil, bake, or fry.

FROG LEGS

Remove legs, skin. Fat content low, flesh firm, flavor delicate. Sauté or fry.

CRAWFISH

Boil whole. Fat content moderate, flesh soft to firm, flavor delicate to mild.

Saltwater Fish

OCEAN PERCH

Skin and draw, fillet, or chunk. Fat content high, flesh firm, flavor moderate. Deep fry, bake, or broil.

BLUEFISH

Skin and draw, fillet, steak, or chunk. Fat content high, flesh firm to soft, flavor moderate. Bake, broil, grill, or smoke.

BUTTERFISH

Fillet or skin and draw. Fat content high, flesh soft to firm, flavor delicate. Smoking is most popular cooking method, but may be fried, baked, or broiled.

COBIA

Skin, fillet, or chunk. Fat content moderate, flesh firm, flavor moderate. Most often deep fried or smoked.

COD

Skin and draw, fillet, steak, or chunk. Fat content low, flesh firm, flavor delicate. Fry, bake, broil, flake into fish cakes, stews or chowder, or smoke.

DRUM, CROAKER, SHEEPSHEAD

Draw and skin, fillet, or chunk. Fat content low, flesh firm, flavor mild. Fry, bake, broil, or smoke.

SEA CATFISH (HARDHEAD)

Skin and draw, fillet, or chunk. Fat content low, flesh soft to firm, flavor mild to strong. Deep fry, smoke, or bake.

FLOUNDER

Skin and draw, fillet, or chunk. Fat content low, flesh firm, flavor delicate. Fry, bake whole, broil, or poach.

TURBOT (GREENLAND)

Fillet or draw. Fat content low, flesh firm, flavor delicate. Fry, bake, broil, or poach.

HADDOCK

Skin and draw, fillet, or chunk. Fat content low, flesh firm, flavor mild. Fry, bake, broil, flake into fish cakes, stews or chowder, or smoke.

HALIBUT

Skin and draw or steak. Fat content low, flesh firm, flavor delicate. Fry, bake, broil, poach, or grill.

LINGCOD

Skin and draw, fillet or steak. Fat content low, flesh firm, flavor delicate. Fry, bake, or smoke.

MACKEREL

Skin and draw, fillet, or steak. Fat content high, flesh firm, flavor strong. Deep fry or smoke.

DOLPHIN (MAHI MAHI)

Skin and draw, fillet, or steak. Fat content moderate, flesh firm, flavor mild. Fry, bake, broil, or grill.

MULLET

Skin and draw, or fillet. Fat content high, flesh firm, flavor mild to strong. Broil, grill, or smoke.

POLLOCK

Skin and draw, fillet, steak, or chunk. Fat content moderate, flesh firm, flavor mild. Fry, bake, or smoke.

POMPANO

Skin and draw, or fillet. Fat content moderate, flesh firm, flavor delicate. Bake, roast in paper bag (*pomillote*), fry, or broil.

PORGY

Skin and draw, or fillet. Fat content low, flesh firm, flavor delicate. Fry, score to cut small bones, and grill.

REDFISH

Skin and draw, fillet, whole, or chunk. Fat content low, flesh firm, flavor mild. Blacken, deep fry, or bake.

RED GROUPER

Skin and draw, chunk, fillet, or steak. Fat content low, flesh firm, flavor mild. Fry, bake, broil, or grill.

RED SNAPPER

Skin and draw, or fillet. Fat content low, flesh firm, flavor mild. Fry, bake, or broil.

ROCKFISH (PACIFIC SNAPPER)

Skin and draw or fillet. Fat content low, flesh firm, flavor mild. Fry, bake, or broil.

SALMON

Draw, fillet or steak. Fat content moderate to high, flesh firm, flavor rich. Grill, bake, poach, or smoke.

SEA TROUT

Skin and draw, fillet, or whole. Fat content moderate, flesh firm, flavor delicate. Fry, bake, poach, or broil.

SEA BASS

Skin or scale, draw, fillet, or chunk. Fat content moderate, flesh firm, flavor delicate. Fry, bake, or poach.

SHAD (AMERICAN)

Draw, whole, or fillet. Fat content high, flesh firm, flavor mild. Bake to soften bones.

SHARK

Draw, fillet, or steak. Fat content low, flesh extremely firm, flavor mild. Grill or broil.

SNOOK

Skin, draw, fillet, or whole. Fat content moderate, flesh firm, flavor mild. Fry, bake, broil, or poach.

SOLE

Skin, draw, fillet, or chunk. Fat content low, flesh fine, flavor delicate. Fry, bake, or broil.

SWORDFISH

Skin, draw, or steak. Fat content moderate, flesh firm, flavor mild. Grill or broil.

SKATES AND RAYS

Skin out wings. Fat content moderate, flesh firm, flavor strong. Boil or fry.

TUNA

Draw, skin, steak, or fillet. Fat content high, flesh firm, flavor mild to rich. Sushi, broil, bake, or pressure can.

WHITING

Draw, skin, steak, fillet, or chunk. Fat content low, flesh firm, flavor mild. Fry, broil, or bake.

Fish Recipes

FISH BATTERS

Frying is probably the most popular method of preparing fish. Following are a number of different batter recipes that can be used for pan frying or deep frying. Some of the batters would also work for oven frying.

BASIC FISH DIP

1 small can evaporated milk (not sweetened)
1 egg
½ cup yellow cornmeal
½ cup flour
1 teaspoon salt
½ teaspoon white pepper

Mix the evaporated milk and egg together with a wire whip. Combine the cornmeal, flour, salt, and pepper. Pat the fish dry, dip in the egg/milk mixture, then roll or shake in the cornmeal mixture. Coated fish may be oven baked, pan-fried or deep-fried. Additional spices may be added as desired.

EGG DIP

3 eggs
1 cup milk
1 teaspoon salt
1 teaspoon pepper
Bread crumbs

Whip the eggs with a wire whip and gradually pour in the milk, salt, and pepper. Pat fish dry, dip in the egg mixture, then roll in bread crumbs. Fish can be baked in a greased casserole dish, pan fried, or deep fried.

SOUR CREAM DIP

1 8-ounce carton dairy sour cream
Bread or cracker crumbs

Stir the sour cream to blend and soften. Pat dry fish fillets, dip in the sour cream, then pat bread or cracker crumbs into the sour cream. This coating is rather soft and is better baked or very carefully pan fried.

SPICY FRIED FISH COATING

½ cup cornmeal
½ cup flour
1 teaspoon garlic salt
1 teaspoon cayenne pepper
1 teaspoon salt

Stir the ingredients together. Roll or shake fish fillets in the coating. A coffee can with a plastic lid makes a great coating container to shake fish in. Deep fry fish to a golden brown in a fish fryer, deep skillet, or Dutch oven. This coating recipe can be doubled or tripled and kept in a tightly closed container for use as needed. The amount of cayenne pepper can be adjusted to suit your family. This spicy coating is great for some of the stronger flavored fish.

BEER BATTER

1 cup beer
2 cups biscuit mix
2 eggs

Whip together the biscuit mix, beer, and eggs until smooth. Pat dry fish fillets and dip in batter. Deep fry to a golden brown.

BUTTERMILK BATTER

1 cup buttermilk
½ cup flour

Whip together the buttermilk and flour. Dip fish fillets in the batter, then in your favorite dry mix such as cornmeal and flour, bread crumbs, cracker meal, or crushed cereals such as corn flakes or rice crisp.

FRIED FISH

DEEP-FRIED FISH BITES

1 pound fish fillets cut into one-inch strips
¼ cup raspberry vinaigrette salad dressing
¾ cup flour
½ teaspoon baking soda
½ teaspoon salt
¾ cup milk, buttermilk or beer
Oil for frying

Pour the salad dressing over the fish pieces and marinate in the refrigerator at least 30 minutes. Meanwhile, mix the flour, baking soda, salt, and liquid. Pat dry the marinated fish pieces and dip in the batter. Deep fry at 375 degrees F. until golden brown. Drain on paper towels. Serve with tartar sauce or shrimp sauce for dipping. These make great appetizers.

PAN-FRIED FISH CAKES

1 pint canned fish, drained and any skin or backbone removed
2 eggs
1 tablespoon lemon juice or vinegar
1 tablespoon grated onion
20 or so crushed saltine crackers

Place the drained fish into a two-quart bowl and mash the bones with a fork. Remove any skin and bones too large to easily mash. Beat the eggs and stir into the fish. Add the lemon juice and grated onion and mix well. Stir in enough crushed saltine crackers to absorb the liquid and to make the mixture stiff enough to form patties. Shape into patties and fry over medium heat in about ¼ inch of oil in a heavy-bottomed skillet. Carefully turn the patties to brown both sides. Serve with tartar sauce as a main dish along with pan-fried potatoes or serve on buns with lettuce, tomato and tartar sauce. Note: These fish cakes are made extra quick and easy in the food processor. Start with the lemon juice, add a chunk of onion, and process until the onion is pureed. Add the drained fish and eggs and whip just a second to mix, then add the crackers a few at a time until the mixture reaches the right consistency to form patties.

FISH CUTLETS

1 cup canned fish, drained and flaked, large bones removed and
   small ones mashed with a fork
2 tablespoons butter or margarine
4 tablespoons flour
½ cup milk
2 tablespoons finely chopped green pepper
1 tablespoon lemon juice (if the fish was canned with vinegar or
   lemon juice, do not add more)
Salt and pepper to taste
1 egg, beaten
Bread crumbs or cracker crumbs
Oil

Melt butter in a saucepan, stir in flour, then add milk and cook
until thick. Stir in the flaked fish, green pepper, salt and pepper, and
lemon juice. Mix well and form into patties. Refrigerate the patties
for an hour or so to firm. Dip each patty in the beaten egg then in
the crumbs and fry in hot oil until brown.

HUSH PUPPIES

Recipes for hush puppies are as varied as fish recipes. Following is a basic version that is fairly plain along with some additions
that take it to hot and spicy. Hush puppies can also be made with
all cornmeal and no flour or half and half cornmeal and flour. White
cornmeal can also be substituted for the yellow.

½ cup self-rising flour
1 cup yellow self-rising cornmeal
½ teaspoon salt
⅛ teaspoon garlic powder
⅛ teaspoon white pepper
2 tablespoons finely chopped onion
1 egg
¼ to ½ cup milk, evaporated milk or buttermilk

Mix the flour, cornmeal, salt, garlic and pepper. Mix the egg into
the milk and stir into the flour mixture. Add more milk if needed to
make a fairly stiff mixture. Stir in the onion. Drop by spoon into hot
oil and cook until the hush puppies float to the surface. If hush

puppies aren't as light and fluffy as you would like, add milk a little at a time.

Any of the following can be added to the above recipe:

¼ cup corn
½ teaspoon to 2 tablespoons sugar or brown sugar
1 teaspoon ground sage
¼ cup chopped green chilies or 1 or more chopped jalapeño peppers or ⅛ teaspoon or more ground cayenne pepper
¼ cup finely chopped sweet green pepper

BAKED FISH

BAKED CATFISH FILLETS

1 8-ounce carton french onion sour cream dip
1½ to 2 cups crushed potato chips
4 catfish fillets

This recipe is very good for larger catfish fillets. Dry the fillets with paper towels. Using the back of a tablespoon or spatula, spread the french onion dip on one side of a fillet and dip that side in the crushed chips. Place, dipped side down in a well-greased baking dish, spread sour cream on the top side and pat with crushed chips. Prepare the remainder of the fillets in the same manner. Bake in a 375 degree F. oven for 25 to 30 minutes depending on the thickness of the fillets or until the fish flakes easily.

BAKED WHOLE CATFISH

4 small, pan-size catfish
salt and pepper
½ stick butter or margarine
1 to 1½ cups crushed saltine crackers, cheese crackers or fine bread crumbs

Melt the butter in a glass baking dish in the oven or microwave. Dip each catfish in the butter, lightly salt and pepper the fish, then pat with crumbs and place back in the baking dish. Pat any leftover crumbs on top of the fish. Bake uncovered in a 375 degree F. oven until the fish flakes and the crumbs are crisp and brown. Note: If using crushed potato chips, add only pepper to the fish. (Most potato chips will add more than enough salt to the fish.) This is one of the easiest and best tasting recipes for small catfish.

DOBBINS BAKED WHOLE CATFISH

This similar recipe comes from my longtime fishing friend Scrappy Dobbins.

4 fresh catfish, skinned, heads, fins, and intestines removed.
½ cup vegetable oil
25 saltine crackers, crushed
salt and pepper to taste

Wash, drain and pat dry catfish. Season with salt and pepper. Roll fish in oil, making sure it is completely covered, then roll in cracker crumbs, coating thoroughly. Place on a cookie sheet or baking dish and bake for 1 hour and 15 minutes at 325 degrees F., or until flesh flakes.

SOUR CREAM BAKED FISH FILLETS

1 pound of fish fillets (bass, crappie, walleye, perch, or any white-fleshed saltwater fish)
Italian dressing
½ cup real mayonnaise
1 cup sour cream
½ cup onion, finely chopped or grated
Italian bread crumbs
Lemon pepper, to taste
Dash paprika

Marinate the fish fillets in the bottled dressing in the fridge for an hour or so. Drain the excess marinade from the fillets, then roll them in the Italian bread crumbs. Arrange the fillets in a single layer in a lightly buttered baking dish and sprinkle with lemon pepper. Combine sour cream, mayonnaise and onion and pour over fish. Garnish the top with a light sprinkling of paprika and bake at 400 degrees F. for 15 to 20 minutes or until light brown and bubbly and the fish flakes.

EASY BAKED SALMON

Salmon fillet
Lemon pepper
Garlic salt
Butter

Place the salmon fillet skin side down in a well-greased baking dish. Brush the top of the salmon with butter and sprinkle with lemon pepper and garlic salt. Bake in a 375 degree F. oven until the fish flakes easily when tested with a fork. Very easy and very good.

LACQUERED SALMON

The following is an excellent recipe that I cajoled from Scott Johnson, the cook at Saltery Lake Lodge on Kodiak Island, Alaska.

2 cups soy sauce
2 tablespoons cornstarch
2 tablespoons sesame oil
2 tablespoons minced ginger
2 tablespoons rice wine or dry sherry
1 tablespoon honey
1 tablespoon Tabasco
1 teaspoon black pepper
4 garlic cloves, chopped
½ teaspoon ground turmeric
2 bunches green onion, whole
1 bunch green onion, chopped
8 (8 ounce) salmon fillets

Lightly oil a baking dish. Add the salmon and whole scallions. Make a sauce by stirring together the first 10 ingredients and pour ½ of the sauce over the fish. Bake until the salmon is just baked through, approximately 20 minutes, basting frequently with remaining sauce and adding ⅓ cup water if sauce begins to burn. Garnish with chopped green onions.

BAKED ITALIAN FISH

1 small onion, thinly sliced
1 clove garlic, diced
⅛ teaspoon crushed basil
Oil
1 can tomato soup, undiluted
1 pound fish fillets
Salt and pepper
Grated cheese

Simmer the onion, garlic, and basil in a small amount of oil in an oven-proof skillet. When the onion and garlic are transparent, stir in the tomato soup. Salt and pepper the fish fillets, add the fillets to the skillet pushing them down into the soup mixture. Bake in a 350 degree F. oven for 20 to 25 minutes depending on the thickness of the fillets. Sprinkle grated cheese over each fillet and return to the oven until the cheese is melted and the fillets flake easily. Serve the fillets and sauce over fettuccini.

EASY-DOES-IT BAKED FISH

Place whole fish or a single layer of fillets in a baking dish. Add milk to almost cover. Place pats of butter over the fish and salt and pepper to taste. Lemon pepper adds flavor, as does paprika. Bake for 15 to 20 minutes at 400 degree F.

OVEN-FRIED FISH

Fish fillets or whole, pan-sized fish
½ cup flour
1 teaspoon salt
½ teaspoon white pepper
1 large egg
3 tablespoons water
1 cup corn flake crumbs
⅓ cup grated Parmesan cheese
½ stick margarine, melted

Pat the fish dry then roll in the flour mixed with the salt and pepper. Whip the egg with the water. Stir the cheese into the corn flake crumbs. Dip the floured fish in the egg mixture then in the corn flake crumbs. Brush the inside of a baking dish with margarine and place the fish in the dish. Pour the rest of the melted margarine over the fish and bake in a 375 degree F. oven until the fish flakes and the coating is brown and crispy.

STUFFED FILLETS

1 package cornbread stuffing mix
Fish fillets, long and thin
Salt and pepper
1 can cream of mushroom soup
½ cup sour cream
½ cup milk

Prepare the stuffing mix according to package directions. Salt and pepper each fish fillet and spread a layer of stuffing on each. Roll the fillets up jellyroll style and secure ends with a toothpick. Place the fillets in a greased baking dish. Stir together the soup, sour cream, and milk and pour over and around the fillets. Bake covered at 375 degrees F. for 20 to 25 minutes. Uncover and finish baking until fish is flaky.

If you don't have large fish fillets to make the stuffed rolls, this recipe can be made into a simple casserole. Spread the stuffing mix in a greased casserole and place the fish fillets on top of the stuffing. Pour the soup mixture over all and bake.

MICROWAVE FISH

ITALIAN FILLETS

6 or 8 fish fillets
Bottled Italian salad dressing
Lemon pepper

Place the fish fillets in a single layer in a well buttered microwave safe dish. Pour a little Italian dressing over each fillet and sprinkle with lemon pepper. Cover the dish with microwave-safe plastic wrap and refrigerate an hour or so. Fold one corner of the plastic wrap back to let steam escape and microwave on high for four to eight minutes depending on the thickness of the fillets, the microwave and how tightly packed the fillets are in the dish. Turn the dish often or cook on a turntable.

EASY MICROWAVE FILLETS

1 pound fish fillets
Garlic salt
Lemon pepper
½ to 1 stick margarine
Chopped fresh or dried parsley

Melt butter in a microwave safe dish to about ½ inch deep. Dip each fillet into the butter and turn over to coat both sides of each fillet with butter. Sprinkle each fillet with garlic salt and lemon pepper and garnish with a little parsley. Cover the dish with microwave safe plastic wrap, folding back one corner of the covering to let steam escape. Microwave on high for four to eight minutes depending on the thickness of the fillets, the microwave, and how tightly packed the fillets are in the dish. Turn the dish often or cook on a turntable.

POACHED FISH

WINE POACHED FILLETS

1 pound fish fillets, mild and white-meated fish
Italian dressing
Dash Tabasco sauce
1 cup white wine
¼ cup water
Garlic salt
Lemon pepper
Cornstarch

Add tabasco sauce to the Italian dressing to taste and brush on the fish fillets. Allow to marinate for at least 30 minutes. Sprinkle the fillets with garlic salt and lemon pepper. Place the fillets in a large skillet, pour the wine and water around the fillets and poach for approximately five to fifteen minutes depending on the thickness of the fillets or until fish flakes easily. Carefully remove the fillets to a warm platter. Reduce the liquid in the skillet, then stir a little cornstarch into the skillet and cook until thickened. Spread the sauce over the fillets and serve immediately.

LEMON POACHED FILLETS

1 to 2 pounds fish fillets
1 small onion, thinly sliced
1 lemon, thinly sliced (remove any seeds)
Salt and pepper, to taste
Water

Place the sliced onions and lemons in the bottom of a large skillet. Place the fish fillets over the lemon and onion slices. Salt and pepper the fillets. Pour water around the fillets and poach for five to fifteen minutes or until fish flakes.

GRILLED FISH

GRILLED SALMON STEAKS

4 salmon steaks
Basting Sauce:
½ cup grated onion
½ cup melted butter
¼ cup lemon juice
Salt and pepper to taste

Place the steaks on the grill and baste with the combined sauce ingredients. Cook over medium coals for ten minutes. Turn, baste and cook for an additional ten minutes or until fish flakes. Garnish with parsley.

GRILLED FISH STEAK WITH ALMOND SAUCE

3 pounds fish steak from any large, white-meated fish
Almond Sauce:
⅔ cup almonds, blanched
1 tablespoon butter
¾ cup cream
½ teaspoon onion salt
dash of paprika

Grill steak five minutes to a side, basting with melted butter. Grill until fish flakes easily.

Sauce: Food process, slice or dice the almonds then brown in butter in a non-stick skillet. Stir in cream and onion salt. Cook over a low flame, stirring constantly until mixture thickens. Add a dash of paprika, then serve over grilled steak.

GRILLED BASS

Any large, white-meated fish fillets will suffice.
Sauce:
¼ pound butter
1 tablespoon Worcestershire sauce
1 teaspoon salt
½ teaspoon pepper
¼ cup lemon juice

In saucepan melt butter and add other sauce ingredients. Use barbeque brush to apply sauce to both sides of the fillets. Place fillets in wire fish-grilling basket. Grill over medium coals three to five minutes per side, turning and basting as you cook.

GRILLED FISH FILLETS WITH HORSERADISH SAUCE

1 pound fish fillets (bass, walleye, catfish crappie, or white-flesh saltwater fillets)
Italian dressing or favorite bottled marinade
4 tablespoons butter or margarine
2 tablespoons white horseradish
2 teaspoons minced fresh parsley
Salt
Lemon pepper
Lemon, thin sliced

Marinate the fish fillets in the Italian dressing or bottled marinade in the refrigerator for an hour or so. Drain the marinade from the fillets and sprinkle with salt and lemon pepper. Place in a fish-grilling basket and grill over charcoal grill or campfire coals three to five minutes to a side. Baste with additional Italian dressing.

Sauce: Heat butter in a microwave safe dish until warm. Stir in horseradish. Spoon warm sauce over fillets and garnish with parsley and sliced lemons.

EASY CAMPFIRE TROUT

Trout, whole, cleaned with skin, and with or without head
Salt and pepper
Bacon
Aluminum foil

Salt and pepper the inside of each trout and wrap in two or more slices of bacon depending on the size of the trout. Wrap each trout in aluminum foil, sealing edges. Place over hot coals and turn frequently to cook evenly. Check after approximately 20 minutes to see if the fish flakes.

GRILLED TROUT

Trout, whole, cleaned with skin, and with or without head
Salt and pepper
Barbecue sauce or garlic butter

Salt and pepper the inside of each trout and place over hot coals. Baste frequently in barbecue sauce or garlic butter and turn several times. Cook until fish flakes easily.

STUFFED TROUT

4 small dressed trout
4 slices bacon
salt and pepper
melted butter
1 cup sliced mushrooms, fresh or canned
¼ cup sweet green pepper, finely chopped
¼ cup celery, finely chopped
¼ cup onion, finely chopped
1 or 2 cloves garlic, finely chopped or crushed

Brush the trout inside and out with melted butter and salt and pepper. In a small skillet brown the vegetables in a small amount of butter. Stuff the cavity of each trout with the vegetables and wrap one strip of bacon around to help hold the trout and stuffing together. Place trout in a greased, hinged wire rack and cook over hot coals approximately 10 minutes per side or until fish flakes. Trout can also be placed in a greased baking dish and baked at 375 degrees F. until fish flakes.

GRILLED SWORDFISH STEAKS

6 swordfish steaks, about 6 ounces each, cut 1-inch thick (Other firm-fleshed fish steaks, such as halibut, tuna, shark, marlin, sturgeon, or even sea bass may be substituted.)
Raspberry vinaigrette dressing
1 large clove garlic, peeled and minced (or crushed)
Dash cayenne pepper

In a small mixing bowl, whisk together the dressing, garlic, and cayenne pepper. Place swordfish steaks in a large, zippered plastic bag. Pour marinade over the fish, seal the bag, and turn to coat fish thoroughly. Refrigerate at least one hour, turning several times. Oil cooking grid and preheat grill on high. Place fish on cooking grid and immediately reduce temperature to medium. Grill five to six minutes. With spatula, turn fish and brush with marinade. Cook another five to six minutes until fish is opaque in the center.

SOUPS AND CHOWDERS

CREAMY FISH CHOWDER

1 to 2 pounds whole dressed fish
2 cups onion, diced
4 to 6 slices bacon
3 to 4 medium potatoes, diced
2 tablespoons butter or margarine
2 tablespoons flour
2 to 3 cups milk or light cream
Salt and pepper

Salt and pepper the fish and simmer in water just until fish flakes from the bones. Do not overcook the fish. Remove the fish from the bones. Strain the broth to remove any bones. Dice the potatoes, cover with salted water and simmer until tender. Drain potatoes. Dice bacon and brown with onions. In a large, heavy-bottomed stock pot, melt the butter and stir in flour. Gradually stir in two to three cups of strained fish stock and cook until thickened. Add the flaked fish, potatoes, bacon and onions, and the milk or cream as needed to bring the soup to the desired consistency. Heat through, adding salt and pepper to taste. This chowder is good served with a few drops of Tabasco sauce and garnished with shredded Swiss or grated Parmesan cheese.

FISH CHOWDER WITH TOMATOES

8 to 10 slices bacon, diced
1 pound fish fillets, diced
½ cup diced onion
4 cups diced potatoes
4 cups water
2 cans diced tomatoes
salt and pepper
1 pint light cream or milk

In a large Dutch oven, fry the bacon. Add the onion and cook until transparent. Add the diced potatoes, water, and salt and pepper. Cook until the potatoes are almost tender, adding more water if needed. Stir in the diced tomatoes and fish and cook over a low flame until the fish flakes. Salt and pepper to taste and stir in cream, heat through and serve.

QUICK FISH CHOWDER

3 cans cream of potato soup
1 can cream of celery, mushroom or chicken soup
3 soup cans milk or part water
4 fish fillets, diced
Salt and pepper, to taste
1 tablespoon butter
1 small onion, diced

Brown the diced onion in the butter in a four-quart saucepan. When the onions are transparent, add the diced fish fillets, salt and pepper and water to almost cover fish. Poach the fish until the meat flakes easily. Stir in the cans of soup and slowly add the milk to the desired consistency. Heat through and serve garnished with shredded cheese. Note: Leftover cooked fish can also be used and added directly to the canned soup.

FISH CASSEROLES

ORIENTAL CASSEROLE

1 to 2 cups cooked flaked fish, crab, or lobster, or a combination
1 can mushroom soup
½ cup sour cream
¼ cup milk
¼ cup finely minced onion
½ cup chopped cashews
1 small can sliced mushrooms, drained
1 can sliced water chestnuts, drained
½ cup finely diced celery
1 package oriental flavor Ramen noodles, crushed

Blend together the mushroom soup, sour cream, milk, and seasoning package from the noodles. Stir in the flaked seafood, vegetables, and cashews, then stir in the crushed noodles. Place in a greased casserole and bake at 350 degrees F. for 30 to 40 minutes or until bubbly and brown and the noodles tender.

SALMON LOAF

2 cups cooked, flaked salmon *or*
1 pint salmon, drained and flaked
1 tablespoon lemon juice
1 can cream of mushroom soup
½ cup milk
½ teaspoon salt
1 beaten egg
½ cup finely chopped celery
1 cup dry bread crumbs

Add lemon juice to salmon. Stir in soup, milk, salt, celery, and bread crumbs and mix well. Bake in greased baking dish in a 350 degree F. oven until brown, about 30 minutes.

TUNA CASSEROLE

1 8-ounce package noodles, cooked and drained
1 can peas, drained
1 can cream of mushroom soup
1 small can diced pimientos
1 half-pint tuna (or other canned fish), drained
1 cup grated cheese
Salt to taste
Bread crumbs and additional grated cheese

Mix ingredients together and place in a well-greased casserole dish. Top with bread crumbs and additional grated cheese and bake in a 350-degree F. oven until brown and bubbly.

SCALLOPED SALMON

1 pint salmon or other canned fish, drained
½ cup finely chopped ripe olives
¾ cup bread crumbs
¾ cup grated cheese
1 tablespoon melted butter
Sauce:
1 cup milk
¼ cup flour
¼ cup butter
Salt and pepper, to taste
1 tablespoon grated onion
1 tablespoon chopped parsley

Prepare the sauce by melting the butter, stirring in the flour, then adding the milk and cooking until thickened. Add salt and pepper, onion and parsley.

In a well-greased baking dish place half of the salmon. Sprinkle over the salmon, half of the ripe olives, bread crumbs, and grated cheese. Pour half of the sauce over the salmon layer. Continue with the remainder of the ingredients and top with buttered bread crumbs. Bake in 350 degree F. oven 30 minutes or until brown and bubbly and the cheese is melted.

APPETIZERS AND SPREADS

DEEP-FRIED FISH BALLS

1 pound fish fillets
4 tablespoons finely ground onion
2 tablespoons oil
½ teaspoon salt
2 tablespoons cornstarch
1 egg
2 teaspoons white wine
Frying oil

Clean and pat the fish dry. Food process a little onion until you have 4 finely ground tablespoons. Add the fish to the processor and grind. Add the next five ingredients and process until smooth. Shape into one-inch balls and deep fry in oil until golden brown. Drain on paper towels. These make great appetizers served with a shrimp or tartar sauce.

CRAB SPREAD

1 8-ounce package cream cheese
½ cup mayonnaise
¼ cup onion, finely diced
¼ cup celery, finely diced
Dash Tabasco and lemon juice
1 cup flaked crabmeat

Soften the cream cheese to room temperature and stir in the mayonnaise. Stir in the finely diced vegetables and add a dash of lemon juice and Tabasco. Stir in the crabmeat. Serve in a bowl as a spread for crackers or mold as below and serve surrounded with crackers.

SMOKED SALMON SPREAD

1 8-ounce package cream cheese
1 cup smoked salmon, flaked
Dash of tabasco sauce

Soften the cream cheese to room temperature. Remove all bones from the salmon and separate into flakes. Mix the cream cheese and salmon and add a few drops of Tabasco sauce to taste. Line a small bowl with plastic food wrap and pack the salmon mixture into the bowl. Chill until firm. Serve by inverting the bowl in the center of a serving platter, carefully remove the plastic wrap, and surround with crackers of your choice.

LOBSTER

Lobster can be cooked whole, or just the tails cooked. A number of methods may be used. With live lobsters heat enough salted water to cover to a boil. Place the lobster in the boiling water. Bring the water back to a boil, then turn down the heat and simmer for about 15 to 20 minutes, or until the crustaceans turn bright red. Remove the lobster with tongs. Position it on its back and using a sharp knife make a cut lengthwise. Take out the black vein that runs to the end of the tail. Remove and discard all other intestines except the brownish-green liver and red coral roe (found only in females). Crack the claws and the lobster is ready to serve. Serve with melted butter to which a bit of lemon has been added.

For frozen rock lobster tails, place in salted boiling water. Bring back to a boil and simmer three to ten minutes depending on size of the tail.

Lobster may also be broiled. First, kill the lobster by making a cut between the tail segment and the body. Split the lobster lengthwise. Remove the entrails, coral or fat and the black vein in the end of the tail segment. Wash the lobster, brush butter on the flesh and salt and pepper to suit. Broil the lobster flesh side down for about ten minutes. Turn the lobster over and broil for another ten minutes.

GRILLED LOBSTER KABOBS

1½ pounds lobster meat, cubed
½ cup olive oil
½ cup white wine
Fresh mushrooms
Cherry tomatoes
Green pepper wedges
Yellow pepper wedges
Sweet onion wedges

Marinate lobster meat in oil and wine. Skewer lobster cubes, alternating with mushrooms, tomatoes, pepper and onion wedges. Brush with olive oil, and salt and pepper to taste. Grill until lobster meat is brown.

OYSTERS

The easiest method of cooking oysters is to broil them in their shells until they open. Then simply drop a bit of butter on them, season with pepper and eat.

DEEP-FRIED OYSTERS

2 cups large, fresh oysters
1 cup crumbs, cornmeal or favorite batter
1 egg, beaten
1 tablespoon milk
Salt and pepper

Rinse and drain oysters. Roll in crumbs or meal. Add the milk and salt and pepper to the egg. Dip the oysters in the egg mixture, then back in the crumbs or meal. Fry in hot oil for just a few minutes until brown.

SCALLOPED OYSTERS

3 cups oysters
Salt and pepper, to taste
3 cups saltine cracker crumbs
½ cup butter or margarine, melted
Approximately ¾ cup milk or light cream
¼ cup finely diced or grated onion
½ cup grated cheese

Strain the liquid from the oysters and add to the milk to make one cup liquid. Combine the crumbs and melted butter. Layer oysters, two cups of the cracker crumbs, onion and cheese in a two-quart buttered casserole. Pour the milk over all. Sprinkle the last cup of crumbs on top and finish with grated cheese. Bake at 350 degrees F. for 45 minutes or until done.

CLAMS

One of the most popular uses of clams is clam chowder. Before clams are open, the first step is to wash the clams while in their shells. Cover the clams with salt water and scrub. Change the water at least twice, scrubbing until clean. The clams can be steamed, baked, or boiled in the shell. Cook only until the shells open. Once the shells open, remove the clams, then remove the meat from the shells.

CLAM CHOWDER

2 dozen clams
4 to 6 strips of bacon, diced
2 medium onions, diced
4 to 6 potatoes, peeled and diced
Clam liquor
2 cups milk
2 cups coffee cream (half 'n half)
3 tablespoons instant potato flakes

Fry the bacon in a large pot. Add the diced onions and cook until transparent. Add the diced potatoes and water to just cover the potatoes, then cook until the potatoes are tender. While the potatoes are cooking, chop the clams and save the liquor around the clams. Add the clams, liquor, and milk. Heat through, but do not boil or overcook the clams. Stir in the cream and heat through. Instant potato flakes can be added to thicken the chowder.

OLD-FASHIONED CLAM BAKE

The first step is to dig a hole in the ground. Line the hole with flat rocks. Build a fire in the hole and allow it to burn for a couple of hours to heat the rocks, adding more wood as needed. Remove the coals and line the pit with seaweed, corn husks, or dampened leaves. Place split lobsters, washed clams in their shells, and corn in the husks in the pit. Cover with seaweed or a canvas tarp. Pile sand or dirt back over the pit to cover and allow to cook for 30 to 45 minutes.

CRAB

Blue crabs are normally hard-shelled, but become soft-shelled when they molt. One of the most popular methods of cooking crab is "deviled crabs." The crabs are placed in boiling salted water until they turn red. Remove them, take off the back shell and pick out the white meat.

CRABMEAT IN SHELLS

½ cup diced celery
½ cup diced green pepper
½ cup diced onion
1 tablespoon butter or margarine
Salt and pepper
2 cups flaked crabmeat or a mixture of crabmeat, shrimp, and/or
    lobster, diced
1 cup real mayonnaise
Dash Tabasco sauce
Bread, cracker, or cornflake crumbs

Brown the vegetables in butter until tender. Mix together the vegetables and crabmeat with just enough mayonnaise to moisten. Salt and pepper to taste. Add a dash of Tabasco if desired. Pack into shell dishes or back into the crab shells and sprinkle crumbs over the top. Bake in a 350-degree oven F. for about 30 minutes or until brown and bubbly.

CREAMED CRAB

1 can cream of celery soup
½ soup can of milk
¼ cup green pepper, finely diced
1 tablespoon diced pimiento
1 can sliced mushrooms, drained
2 cups flaked crabmeat, or other flaked fish meat
Salt and pepper

In a two-quart saucepan, stir together the cream of celery soup and the milk until smooth. Stir in the remaining ingredients and salt and pepper to taste. Cook over medium heat, stirring constantly until mixture is warm. Serve over biscuits, toast triangles, or in patty shells.

SHRIMP

Most shrimp is purchased, but it is also one of the most popular seafoods, and in some places you can collect your own. When purchased, the size of the shrimp is denoted by the number of shrimp in one pound. Jumbo-sized shrimp will have a 15 to 18 count, average-sized shrimp 26 to 30, and small shrimp 60 or more. Shrimp can be prepared in any number of ways.

OLD-FASHIONED BOILED SHRIMP

The easiest way to prepare shrimp is to purchase a package of shrimp boil and follow the directions on the box. Of course, folks used to make up their own shrimp boil. Following is a basic recipe, but you can add or subtract spices to suit your taste.

1 to 2 pounds shrimp
1 stalk celery
1 onion, sliced
1 bay leaf
1 teaspoon salt
8 to 10 peppercorns
½ to 1 teaspoon dried crushed red pepper
1 quart water

Combine the spices and vegetables with the water in a large pot. Bring to a full boil and let the vegetables cook for a few minutes before adding the washed shrimp. Boil 15 to 20 minutes, drain, and rinse in cold water. Keep shrimp in the refrigerator if you're not serving them immediately.

SHRIMP SCAMPI

1 pound shrimp, precooked and peeled
½ cup butter
¼ cup olive oil
5 gloves garlic
¼ cup minced parsley
2 tablespoons lemon juice
1 teaspoon black pepper

Melt butter in a large skillet. Stir in the olive oil, garlic, parsley, lemon juice, and black pepper. Cook over low heat until the garlic is soft. Add the precooked shrimp and heat through. Serve immediately with rice or pasta.

FISH DIPPING SAUCES

TARTAR SAUCE

1 cup mayonnaise or salad dressing
¼ cup finely chopped sweet pickles or sweet pickle relish
1 tablespoon finely chopped or ground onion *or* 2 teaspoons
    horseradish
½ teaspoon lemon juice

In a small bowl, mix mayonnaise with the pickle relish, onion or horseradish, and lemon juice. Cover and keep chilled until serving.

SHRIMP SAUCE

1 cup catsup
1 tablespoon lemon juice
1 to 2 tablespoons horseradish

In a small bowl stir the lemon juice and horseradish into the catsup. Cover and keep chilled until serving.

JACK'S RED DIPPING SAUCE

This recipe, of course, is from the Jack Daniel Distillery and the sauce would probably taste best made with Jack Daniel's Tennessee Whiskey.

1½ cups catsup
2 tablespoons brown sugar
2 tablespoons Worcestershire sauce
1 teaspoon dry mustard
⅓ cup Jack Daniel's Tennessee Whiskey

Combine catsup, brown sugar, Worcestershire sauce, and dry mustard in a small saucepan. Bring to a boil, stirring occasionally. Stir in the whiskey and simmer five minutes. Refrigerate until serving time and serve as a dipping sauce for fish or shellfish.

Sources

American Angler, 800-98-BLADE, www.quikut.com

Bass Pro Shops, 800-BASS PRO, www.basspro.com

Berkley, Pure Fishing, 877-777-3850, www.purefishing.com

Bradley Technologies Canada Inc., 800-665-4188, www.bradleysmoker.com

Buck Knives, 800-326-2925, www.buckknives.com

Cabela's, 800-237-4444, www.cabelas.com

C & C Outdoors, Keith Sutton, 15601 Mountain Dr., Alexander, AR 72002, www.ccoutdoors.com

Chef'sChoice, EdgeCraft Corp., 800-342-3255, www.chefschoice.com

Craftsman, Sears, 800-377-7414, www.sears.com/craftsman

FoodSaver, Tilia, Inc., 800-777-5452, www.foodsaver.com

Excalibur, 800-875-4254, www.excaliburdehydrator.com

G.A.S.S., Gar Angler's Sportsman's Society, www.garfishing.com

Gerber Legendary Blades, 800-950-6161, www.gerberblades.com

Good-One Smokers, Ron Goodwin Enterprises, 620-726-5281, www.thegood-one.com

Intruder, Inc., 800-553-5129, www.accusharp.com

Katz Knives, 800-848-7084, www.katzknives.com

Kershaw Knives, 800-325-2891, www.kershawknives.com

Luhr-Jensen & Sons, Inc., 800-366-3811, www.luhrjensen.com

Mister Twister, Mepps, 800-637-7703, www.mepps.com

Shimano American Corp., 800-274-4626, www.shimano.com

United Cutlery Brands, 800-548-0835, www.unitedcutlery.com

Index